BLOOD
ON THEIR
HANDS

BLOOD ON THEIR HANDS

The Killing of Ann Chapman

RICHARD COTTRELL

GRAFTON BOOKS

A Division of the Collins Publishing Group

LONDON GLASGOW
TORONTO SYDNEY AUCKLAND

Grafton Books
A Division of the Collins Publishing Group
8 Grafton Street, London W1X 3LA

Published by Grafton Books 1987

British Library Cataloguing in Publication Data
Cottrell, Richard
Blood on their hands: the killing of
Ann Chapman.
1. Chapman, Ann – Assassination
2. Greece – Politics and government –
1967–1974
I. Title
364.1'523'0924   DF853.5.C5

ISBN 0-246-12736-8

Photoset in Linotron Sabon by
Rowland Phototypesetting Ltd
Bury St Edmunds, Suffolk
Made and printed in Great Britain by
Mackays of Chatham, Chatham, Kent

For Edward and Dorothy Chapman, whose faith and persistence never failed, and for Tracy, who made this book possible

Contents

Acknowledgements

The photographs taken at the trial of Nicholas Moundis and at the 're-enactment' of his alleged crime are reproduced by permission of Camera Press. Those of Archbishop Makarios, Turkish troops in Cyprus, Andreas Papandreou and Constantine Karamanlis are from Associated Press. 'The mystery in the Thames' is reproduced by permission of the *Surrey Comet*. The rest are from the collection of Edward Chapman or the author.

Chronology

23 MARCH 1946	Ann Chapman born in Streatham
27 MAY 1967	Greek Army overthrows government
FEBRUARY 1971	Ann joins Radio London
13 MARCH 1971	Army coup in Turkey
11 OCTOBER 1971	Ann leaves for Greece with Olympic Holidays party
15 OCTOBER 1971	She is last seen alive at the Pine Hill Hotel, Kavouri
16 OCTOBER 1971	US Vice-President Spiro Agnew arrives in Athens
15/16 OCTOBER 1971	Ann is murdered
18 OCTOBER 1971	Her body is found
28 AUGUST 1972	Nicholas Moundis is arrested and subsequently accused of Ann's murder
5 APRIL 1973	Moundis' trial opens. He is sentenced to life imprisonment for manslaughter
17 NOVEMBER 1973	Students' rising at Athens Polytechnic
24 NOVEMBER 1973	Senior dictator Papadopoulos is deposed by Ioannides
15 JULY 1974	Sampson coup in Cyprus
20 JULY 1974	Turkish troops land in Cyprus
23 JULY 1974	Greek junta collapses
17 MARCH 1980	Kotsias drowns in river Thames
JUNE 1982	European Parliament Petitions Committee inquiry commences
25 MAY 1984	European Parliament in Strasbourg approves 'The Chapman Report'

STRATEGIC MAP: Cyprus, hanging like a pendant from Turkey, but long claimed by the Greeks as part of a resurgent Hellenic empire. Yet never in history was Cyprus truly Greek — or even a Greek dependency. The solution determined by the United States was a division between the Turkish and Greek communities.

KAVOURI AREA: Ann's body was discovered within walking distance of the Pine Hill Hotel, where she was last seen alive by a member of the Olympic Holidays party. Despite intensive searches by the local police, few significant items among her belongings turned up until days after the finding of her corpse, face down in the scrubland with wrists and ankles tied. David Bowen, the London forensic scientist consulted by Edward Chapman, thought this one of the strangest elements of the story.

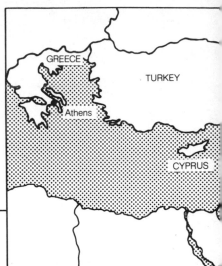

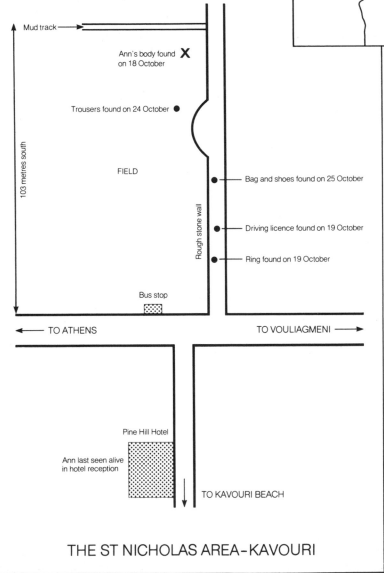

Mud track

Ann's body found **X**
on 18 October

Trousers found on 24 October ●

103 metres south

FIELD

Bag and shoes found on 25 October

Rough stone wall

Driving licence found on 19 October

Ring found on 19 October

Bus stop

◄── TO ATHENS

TO VOULIAGMENI ──►

Pine Hill Hotel

Ann last seen alive
in hotel reception

TO KAVOURI BEACH

THE ST NICHOLAS AREA-KAVOURI

Introduction

Balkan intrigues are always dangerous for the inexperienced. So it proved for Ann Dorothy Chapman. Her young life was snuffed out in a brutal and clumsy fashion in 1971, in the Greece ruled by the Colonels. Her death bequeathed a riddle which her father, with the aid of many investigators, has tried for more than fifteen years to solve. At every stage of his search for the truth, itself a contemporary *Odyssey* in the most noble Greek tradition, Edward Chapman has been deceived by official dishonesty and misled by the wholesale fabrication of lies twisted into an evil contortion of Ann's real fate. Her father, who is now approaching his eightieth year, has become one of the most remarkable pests in the history of independent detection. Quite simply, he has never given up. An engineer by trade, he transformed the gritty realism he brought to his profession into a passion for investigation, spurred by a crusading determination to erase the implicit slur on his daughter's memory — that she was a young woman whose cheap morals led her to the grave. And that, Edward Chapman has so often told me, was a 'filthy abhorrence' to his family.

Practically everyone underestimated the capacity of an aggrieved father to make a nuisance of himself. Edward

Chapman is a remarkable example of self-acquired intelligence. In his late seventies, he remains gaunt, lean-framed and well-endowed with that special variety of acute cynicism which appears to be the inheritance of all true-born south Londoners. But for this appalling tragedy, everything about his sound but mostly unadventurous background indicated a quiet retirement in the evening of his life, tending the roses in his neat suburban semi and enjoying the gentle company of his wife, Dorothy. Instead, Edward Chapman has spent every penny of his retirement investment commuting to and from the country in which his daughter died, challenging governments, ministers, courts and policemen to tell him the truth. From a tiny bedroom converted to an operations centre, an ancient typewriter chattered missives to anyone who would listen or help. Some fifteen years after Ann's death, Edward Chapman has assembled an archive which generously exceeds the harvest of any official investigation of murder. But even the accumulated weight of evidence proved insufficient to achieve the real breakthrough he so desperately sought, that political thrust which would rattle cage bars and frighten the long-silent custodians of the truth.

By 1983, Edward Chapman had grown accustomed to the sound of doors slamming in his face. In that year, as Member of the European Parliament for Bristol, I wrote a chance note to the Chapmans – whom I had never met – telling them of their rights as citizens of the European Community to petition the European Parliament for redress of a grievance against an authority or authorities in another member state. Like almost everyone else in a country which remains supremely agnostic about the European club, the Chapmans knew nothing of this privilege. But Edward Chapman seized upon it immediately, recognizing, as he later declared, 'a heaven-sent opportunity to force the Greeks to tell me the truth'. We subsequently arranged to meet at the London offices of the European Parliament in Queen Anne's Gate. There I proposed to Chapman that he submit a petition to the European Parliament, which would be forwarded automatically to the Petitions Committee which deliberates on the destiny of such documents and adopts the appropriate procedures to achieve redress. This was the birth of European Parliament petition number 13/83 entitled 'Procedures concerning a murder in Greece'. In itself it constituted a unique document. Never before had the European Parliament entertained a petition which contained the potential to challenge the highest legal authority in a member state, for, as the Greeks continued to insist, justice had been done. The Supreme Court, the final arbiter, had concluded that Ann Dorothy Chapman, a British journalist, had met her death during the course of a frustrated sexual encounter with a former prison guard, Nicholas Moundis, who was serving a sentence of life imprisonment.

The petition, when it finally arrived in Brussels, raised political eyebrows. The Greeks, at that time the newest recruits to the EEC, were already suffering from an acute persecution complex brought on by what they considered to be over-enthusiastic criticism of their machinery of state in the wake of signing the Treaty of Rome. To dub the petition admissible would mean setting loose a full parliamentary investigation, which the Greeks were bound to interpret as a slap in the face for a socialist government which, like all others before it, continued to maintain the fiction that every legal opportunity had been exhausted by Ann's father.

My long talks with Edward Chapman, together with my own knowledge of the curious business, naturally led me – as a member of the committee – to introduce the petition. My colleagues were sympathetic but not enthusiastic. They were clearly inclined to shy away from a path which led inevitably towards some kind of constitutional conflict with the Greek state. Some opinions were frankly hostile. 'An old man should be satisfied with what he has been told,' one said. 'He will make himself ill and miserable by going on like this.' But throughout the debate ran a vein of *angst* – that German word is here most appropriate – over this obviously mysterious incident during the fairly recent lifetime of a European military junta which had displayed overtly fascist symbolism. Political nerves jangled, especially those of deputies from the German Social Democratic Party whose old sympathies for the victims of right-wing tyranny swept to the surface. The committee wrestled with the options open to it. I could see that opinion was leaning towards a vote which would result in a decision of 'petition inadmissible' – and that could only mean another letter of polite regrets to the Chapman home in Putney.

Then something remarkable happened in a most unexpected quarter. Among the members of the committee was a deputy from the Greek New Democracy (roughly translated, Conservative) Party. He was Costas Gontikas, an intensely well-groomed, slightly pompous but unusually humorous lawyer from Athens. He sucked quietly at a pipe as the debate rolled on and then raised a hand to indicate that he wished to intervene. After ranging over his extensive knowledge of the affair, he told the committee that, when the vote came, he would abstain. Gontikas was not a 'system politician' – he later fell out with his political masters at home and there is some evidence to suggest that his crucial intervention on that day in Brussels led to him falling foul of the New Democracy leadership. What he said was this: his colleagues should appreciate that virtually everyone in Greece believed Chapman's version of events: that his daughter had been murdered as part of a political conspiracy and that the facts had subsequently been covered up.

The change in atmosphere inside the committee room following Gontikas' statement was electric. A highly loquacious Italian communist, another lawyer holding a potentially vital vote, sprang up to say that he had now changed his mind. If a Greek lawyer suspected a betrayal of justice, that was good enough for him. The vote ensued swiftly. By the narrowest of margins, the committee chose the most adventurous course. It declared the petition admissible and decided to appoint one of its number to conduct the appropriate inquiries, leading to the presentation of a full-scale resolution to Parliament assembled in Strasburg. What then followed was, I suppose, inevitable. The Danish chairman suggested that the Member for Bristol had virtually volunteered for the task. 'Be sure to get yourself a deer-stalker hat and a nice curly pipe,' he joked.

Later that day, BBC news bulletins made a rare reference to the European Parliament, reporting that it had decided to reopen the then twelve-year-old case of the murder of Ann Chapman. Athens reacted at first with a deafening silence and then with a wave of officially-orchestrated protest against this 'interference in the internal affairs of our country'. Within weeks my name was hauled through a mass of disinformation. Many Greek newspapers carried reports designed to discredit the parliamentary inquiry on the grounds that I was an identifiable propagandist and apologist for Turkey, Greece's hated neighbour. Public opinion was encouraged to believe that the inquiry had been set up merely to damage faith in the integrity of the Greek state and, in particular, in its institutions of justice. Where words would not suffice, other means were sought to discourage me.

In 1982–3 I had already troubled the Greek authorities by taking up the case of a young constituent, a foolish girl who had got herself mixed up with drugs and fell into the hands of a bunch of grim policemen in Piraeus, the maritime suburb of Athens. The girl claimed she had been tortured after her arrest by a beating to the soles of her feet. Her claims were sufficiently convincing to warrant an official protest from the British government, in itself a fairly rare event, even more so in the case of an addict who had not actually denied the charges brought against her. She insisted that her tormentors had been inspired by the desire to locate what they believed to be a large cache of drugs for their own use, in underground trade to supplement their income.

This affair took me down many strange alleyways and into corridors below the surface of the Greek state, but it served as an invaluable foretaste of what was yet to come. The girl was eventually released from prison after a series of occasionally almost comic confusions. Once I received a threat to my life unless I left the matter alone. When I started the Chapman investigation, the pressures to desist were far more sinister. During one mission to Greece, a Dutch journalist familiar with the ways of the country warned me bluntly: 'Be careful – strange accidents can happen here. What you are doing is dangerous for many people, and not least yourself.'

I soon had proof of that. The following day, returning to my hotel after a stroll to find some fresh air in the fuggy pollution of the Greek capital, I was confronted at the door by a man who had evidently been waiting in a car. The brief scene which followed was reminiscent of a minor confrontation in Chicago during the gangster era. A man with a neat suit and moustache told me in clearly pronounced English: 'You should understand that you are being very unhelpful in this business of Chapman. My advice to you is to leave Athens now and forget all about it. Otherwise there could be some consequences which you will not like – you understand?' He displayed a row of well-set pearls complete with generous gold fillings. I was about to suggest a more detailed discussion of these 'consequences' in the hotel lobby where a policeman was lounging at the reception desk, when my visitor stepped quickly back into his car, a battered grey Mercedes, and swept off down the narrow street in a cloud of dust. When I entered my room, I found it had been thoroughly but expertly searched. This also happened on two other occasions. That night the telephone in my room rang about a dozen times. There was no heavy breathing, only the merest crackly hint of someone holding the receiver at the other end. The same long arm predictably reached Brussels, where similar annoying calls were made to my flat. The telephone apparatus at home in England acquired a peculiar hollow resonance which is often, I am told, the hallmark of bugging.

More than once those many Greek friends who freely gave help, advice, encouragement and information warned me: 'Always look behind you, Richard. We are not yet a democracy in Greece.' I reckoned, however, that my profile was too high to join the tally of unexplained deaths and disappearances connected with the Chapman affair. But the propaganda war went on, a steady drip of poisonous disinformation and gossip always linking me with that historic obsession of Greece, the fear of Turkish forces sweeping across the Aegean. Because I had argued – quite independently from the Chapman investigation – for a more accurate interpretation of what had really happened in Cyprus, the Greek press liked to portray me as a 'poodle of Ankara and the illegal regime of Denktash in Cyprus'. European curiosity about the internal political situation in Greece registers so low on the awareness scale that few people outside the country comprehend the profound depths of Greek – and Turkish – feeling over the fate of that troubled island. Merely to talk with Turks, or have Turkish Cypriot friends, brands you as a traitor to Hellenic nationalism; yet it proved to be a clumsy error on the part of the Greeks to link the Chapman inquiry and me with the division of Cyprus, another sinister episode about which the Greek people have never been told the truth.

Eventually, when the Greek government could contain its frustrations no longer, it tried to shut me out of the country. In the summer of 1985 I was formally detained at Athens airport after arriving on a plane from Brussels. After several hours incarcerated in a sweaty immigration office, I was informed that I was about to be evicted from the country for the sin of bearing a passport which revealed I had visited the 'Turkish Republic of Northern Cyprus'. It was revealing, that stifling August night, how the passport officer had greeted me by name before he had even inspected the document. I obliged

by offering to arrange an international incident, and invoked
the aid of the British embassy. The row flew all the way to
the desk of the Minister for Public Order, who was forced
grudgingly to quash his own edict that no one who had
consorted with an 'illegal regime' in Cyprus might enter
Greece. The incident created a political storm in Greece,
Turkey and, eventually, Brussels, where the European Commission threatened the Greek government with a full-dress
appearance at the European Court for improperly hindering
the legal passage of an EEC citizen between one member state
and another. The injunction forbidding visitors to northern
Cyprus to enter Greece has no legal basis whatsoever in
international law, and in 1986 it was finally dropped
altogether. But for the Greeks it briefly presented an opportunity of last resort, a chance to slam the door in my face,
just as it had been slammed on Edward Chapman so many
times before.

In May 1984, it was at last the turn of the Greek government to be told the meaning of justice. In the final vote during
the parliamentary session in Strasburg that month, the House
voted, unanimously, to support my finding that Ann had
not been killed by Moundis, whom I declared completely
innocent, and that she was instead the victim of 'agents acting
illegally under the authority of the military regime'. In the
end, Parliament travelled all the way along the road to challenge the highest legal authority in a member state, but
stopped diplomatically short of calling many people in high
places liars. The final resolution, supported by a detailed
report, told a story of consistent deception which the Greek
authorities were urged to correct. Within a few months,
Moundis was released from prison by presidential edict – but
not officially pardoned. By that act it was hoped to stem the
pressure for a full pardon, which would only lead to a new
inquiry to detect Ann's killers and thus, as this book will
reveal, raise other ghosts concerned with the matter of

8

Cyprus. But for the Chapmans it was at last a vindication of what they had always insisted – and at long last that terrible smear of sexual promiscuity was wiped from Ann's name.

Over this long investigation lay the shadow of the young woman who had been strangled fifteen years before. I sometimes feel that perhaps I knew Ann as well as anyone. She was a curious victim of a conspiracy which appeared, by strange alchemy, to have selected her as a victim. To dig deeply into the personality of someone long dead is not as difficult as it might seem. I believe that Ann was herself desperately in search of that personality. The passion for intimate human contact appears to have passed her by completely. She was a young woman who collected acquaintances, rather than forged passionate friendships. She was driven by the motor of ambition, but it hummed so quietly few others detected the sound. For that reason she was too swiftly dismissed as insufficiently motivated. In essence, she was a classic late developer. Had Ann returned from Greece in the early autumn of 1971, I am convinced that something remarkable would have happened to develop her character and personality. Edward and Dorothy Chapman feel that, too. And that is why the pain of being robbed of their daughter is so much the greater.

This book is more than the story of Ann, her brief life and squalid murder. Those who killed her have never been brought to account, although it has always been open to any Greek government since the fall of the Colonels to accomplish that. There has been no single act of compassion, unless one counts the restoration of liberty to Nicholas Moundis. There are people alive in Greece today who bear Ann's blood on their hands. The words from Arthur Conan Doyle which begin this Introduction are singularly appropriate, for the unique appointment of a Member of Parliament as a murder investigator – and for a story which has not yet reached its ending.

1 · The Girl with Stars in her Eyes

Why, what could she have done, being what she is?
Was there another Troy for her to burn?

— W. B. Yeats

The body of Ann Dorothy Chapman, a twenty-five-year-old freelance journalist working for the BBC's newly established Radio London, was found in a field in the St Nicholas district of Vouliagmeni, some twenty kilometres south of Athens, as evening set in on Monday 18 October 1971. She had been strangled. Ann Chapman had gone to Greece on what those who are pleased to follow the craft of journalism like to call a 'freebie', an expenses-paid expedition which, in this case, was aimed primarily at travel agents and intended to promote the tourist industry in a country under the control of a military dictatorship. Four years previously, civilian rule had been extinguished by an army-inspired coup against the youthful, inexperienced Greek monarch, Constantine. Within another three years the rule of the Greek Colonels would end in calamity in the débâcle over Cyprus.

Ann had found her way into broadcasting only a few months before her death through several chance acquaintances, one of whom was Michael Vestey. Now firmly established in the BBC's hierarchy of talent, Vestey told me in 1983 that he had been introduced to Ann by a friend who ran a moderately avant-garde coffee bar, the Troubadour, in

10

the Old Brompton Road. The Troubadour, with its curious brew of people who met there, appears to have been the centre of Ann's social life, since she had few boyfriends and even fewer close friends. Vestey recalled that the Troubadour's owner, Bruce Rogerson, asked him to talk to a young woman who was keen to get into broadcasting. They met at a pub in Hanover Square and he later arranged an introduction to the management at Radio London, which Vestey recommended as an excellent nursery in the still relatively young world of local radio broadcasting. They were by all accounts desperately short of talent and wanted to find freelancers who could be paid 'by the spot'. In Vestey's words: 'They wanted "bodies" – people prepared to show enthusiasm rather than expertise. The skill they hoped would come later.' Vestey went on to encourage Ann, showing her how to use recording equipment and how to develop her interviewing technique. He thought she was shy, and wondered if she would prove assertive enough to succeed in the brittle world of broadcasting. The two remained in touch until she left for Greece.

Michael Vestey remembers that another Radio London veteran, Bob Trevor, heard Ann talking about the trip and saying that she wanted to talk to political prisoners, among them Lady Amelia Fleming, widow of the penicillin pioneer, whose imprisonment by the Greek junta had caused a sensation abroad. Vestey's recollection reveals that Ann had matured in the job quickly. 'I only wished that she had discussed it with me,' he said. 'Though I suspect that her ambition to succeed would have ruled her head and she would have gone ahead with whatever project she had in mind.' He, too, has never believed the story that Ann was attacked and strangled by a virtually illiterate labourer who succeeded in persuading her, despite the language barrier, to step into a field beside a bus stop for a brief sexual encounter. Neither has Brian Hanrahan, another radio cub who subsequently enjoyed national fame after his reporting of the Falklands conflict. Hanrahan had drinks with Ann on several occasions and offered her advice and encouragement. The suggestion that she would strike up a sexual relationship with a total stranger at a bus stop struck Hanrahan as completely out of character with the rather donnish young graduate that he knew. Hanrahan sets Ann and himself perfectly in the capsule of their time, both fresh from university, liberal, a little left-wing, and well-laced with youthful cynicism.

Retired radio engineer Johnnie Longden remembered Ann as modest and unassuming, 'intelligent in a quiet sort of way'. And neither Mike Brook nor Charles Murray, both contemporaries in the newsroom, were satisfied with the official explanation of her death given by the Greek authorities. Both were troubled by an explicit BBC instruction that Ann was not to be described in any broadcast as an employee of the Corporation which, strictly speaking, as a freelance, she was not. Radio London's chaplain of the air at the time was a Methodist minister, the Rev. Eric Blennerhassett. He recalled: 'She was not a flighty sort of girl at all; in fact, rather less forthcoming than the average girl . . . the impression I gained of Ann was of a serious-minded young girl at the start of an interesting and promising career.' In contrast, David Carter, who still works at the station arranging music programmes, declared: 'A dull, boring girl, thick as two short planks, with stars in her eyes. I don't think she was capable of uncovering anything big or international unless someone told her to seek something out and, like a fool, in her naivety she did.'

Certainly the kind of people Ann met at the Troubadour spent long hours talking about politics and the issues of the day. Her flatmate, a young house doctor called Danny Lessing, thought of the coffee bar as 'a lefty place', where 'politics was discussed a lot'. They had shared a home together for only a few weeks before Ann left for Greece, but they had

been friends since their early teens. Despite this long friendship, Danny remembered Ann as 'a bit of a cold fish', who kept
very much to herself and rarely, if ever, displayed emotions.

There was a remarkable lack of passion in Ann's life so far
as men were concerned. Nita de Peterson, a confidante of
Ann's and another regular at the Troubadour, thought that
Ann would consider sex only in the context of a very serious
relationship, and there were few signs of Ann looking for close
entanglements. Ann's diary is full of jottings for appointments
and interviews, and only a scattering of references to social
events. It seems that few of the men she knew made passes
at her. One who has freely admitted trying is Gareth Davis,
then a young radiologist, who now lives in Amsterdam. In
1985 he told me that in the early 70s he was a caricature of
'the young man in medicine'. With other medical friends, he
reaped a rich harvest of young nurses – and it was a convincing
claim, even allowing for middle-age confidence and the ability
of the memory to exaggerate youthful pleasures. Davis met
Ann at Danny Lessing's flat and took her out to dinner four
or five times; four occasions were recorded in her diary. He
says he was attracted to Ann because she was 'different' and
not part of the medical world in which he was enjoying
himself so much. He thought her prim and proper with rather
a 'cold' personality. If they did kiss, he does not recall it as
a passionate experience; nor could he precisely remember
whether or not he went to bed with Ann. Friends now say
that she thought him pompous and he agrees that he probably
was – 'though she did laugh at most of my jokes'. After
Ann's death, Davis found himself the target of considerable
suspicion because he had written in her diary, in Greek, verse
13 from John 15: 'Greater love hath no man than this, that
a man lay down his life for his friends.' Ann's father and
other investigators thought this implied that he knew a good
deal about the motives for Ann's journey, that she may have
been on some kind of political mission which led to her death.

On 1 October 1971, just a few days before she departed for Greece, Ann had arranged to see Gareth Davis, but he now recalls no such meeting. This is odd, because the entry in her diary is in his own very particular handwriting. He does remember Ann saying shortly before she left for Greece that an interview with Amelia Fleming would be a coup for her journalistic career. So why did he choose that curious inscription, in Greek, which he, but not she, could understand? His letter to Edward Chapman in 1973, offering an explanation, now seems deliberately condescending and insensitive. Davis said he had also tried to impress Ann with a demonstration of French acrostics, 'basically amusing little games that the French play – all represent idle doodlings during dinner one evening'. Which, of course, is what they were. He admits that there was probably a degree of smugness and conceit about him at the time, which, inevitably, infuriated the desperate father trying to discover who had really murdered his daughter.

There can be no doubt that Gareth Davis knew nothing about plots or secret missions. His relationship with Ann is, in fact, significant in only one respect: he, potentially the most likely candidate to overcome the girl's natural reserve, did not succeed in doing so. Ann held out against his flattery and charm and told him no more about herself than she had told anyone else.

From my interviews with people like Gareth Davis, and with others who were really acquaintances, never friends, Ann is revealed as a self-contained individual who would keep entirely to herself her real motives for making the voyage that led to her death.

Ann's short, busy life contained few signs of flamboyance. She was born in the south London suburb of Streatham on 23 March 1946. The Chapmans' only daughter, she was six years younger than her brother John who is now married with two children and, like his father, an engineer. Her mother, Dorothy, remembers Ann from her earliest days as 'a marvellous girl, never a day's trouble, always placid, with no temper'. She was sent first to a small private school and then to a local primary before winning a scholarship to Putney High. Ann was the classic all-rounder, studious, nearly always top of the class, fond of tennis, swimming and hockey, and, although shy by nature, never without a group of friends. She enjoyed music and Dorothy Chapman encouraged an interest in ballet at Sadler's Wells, where she passed her dancing exams easily. It was clear that the Chapmans' quietly proficient and happy young daughter was university material and she went on to Manchester University where she received a good degree in psychology. Her links with home were always strong. She and brother John enjoyed long debates over the dinner table and later, when she had left university, often talked politics with her father. Ann had a pronounced dislike, he says, for politicians of the Right like Enoch Powell. She seems to have been the type of graduate who would find a political home on the soft Left. As Nita de Peterson later put it, 'We would have been the SDP people of our time.' With her mother she talked about helping deprived children and indeed later worked briefly for Christian Aid. Ann was bookish, which delighted her mother who could see only a bright and successful future once her daughter had chosen a career. But Ann never talked about using her psychology degree and the search for a career proved elusive.

After getting her degree at Manchester, Ann became a research assistant at the London School of Economics which was, by one of the many coincidences in the Chapman story, already a focus of resistance to the Colonels' seizure of power in Greece. Her boss at the LSE was Professor Frederick Northedge, a key sympathiser with a committee which had been formed, mostly by Hellenophile university academics, to promote opposition in Britain to the Athens military regime. Ann told her father bluntly that she did not like Northedge, who died in 1985.

Professor Northedge had strong links with John Dragoumis, a Greek who became the target of sensational accusations in the wake of Ann's death. Northedge and his wife had spent a holiday with Dragoumis on the Aegean island of Poros in 1967, the year the Colonels seized power. Dragoumis was active in the resistance movement inside Greece itself, using as cover a small language school he ran on Poros. He is now remembered by everyone involved with the resistance as a very peculiar figure. When an article in the *Daily Express* accused him of betraying the resistance as a double-agent, he sued for libel and won. In 1985, Northedge recalled one typically strange incident with Dragoumis during the Poros holiday: the pair scaled a mountain to find a secret hideout where Dragoumis could evade junta agents. They remained friendly throughout and long after the junta years.

We cannot be sure exactly why Ann took a dislike to Northedge, but it was almost certainly here at the LSE that she tapped into his links with the anti-junta groups and found her curiosity roused by what was going on in Greece, a curiosity fed by her own natural liberal sympathies and an equally natural dislike of all that the Colonels represented.

Desire for a change then took Ann to Paris for a year, where she shared a flat with an English girl and taught at the Berlitz School of Languages. There were no obvious signs of any 'Bohemian' influence on Ann, except that she started to use pot occasionally in a mild way, a habit which she later indulged in with Nita de Peterson in London. One or two of the Troubadour's customers had access to cannabis but nothing harder, and by all accounts Ann had strong views on hard drugs. Her occasional use of pot is almost the only indication of anything slightly risqué in the behaviour of this otherwise remarkably serious young woman. Yet drugs became significant after her death. There were persistent

16

reports, circulated with official encouragement, that drugs had been found in her suitcase and also that she had had a row about drugs with a young travel courier who refused to share a room with her after a 'clash of personalities'. Edward Chapman declares that he knows nothing about his daughter smoking pot and regards it as another blatant attempt by the Greek authorities to smear her name. The Chapmans were not in any case the kind of people whose unassuming suburban life would bring them into contact with such exotica, and Ann knew her parents well enough to keep quiet about something which would obviously disturb them. If there really were traces of cannabis in her suitcase at the hotel in which she was staying at the time of her death, it is surprising that the police officers who searched her room and then scooped up the scattered belongings around her body failed to make any reference to such a potentially significant find in their detailed inventory. The story does, however, fit in with the theory that a desperate attempt was made to smear Ann's name to match the official version of events: a flighty young foreigner looking for quick sex who fell into the hands of Nicholas Moundis.

After Paris, Ann's appetite for adventure was fed by a long trek to India and Katmandu, returning home through Afghanistan and the Middle East. In order not to worry her parents Ann said she had flown throughout the entire trip, whereas in fact she had spent much of it travelling overland, on one occasion sunbathing on the beach in Goa with an Indian who now works at the European Commission in Brussels. Their main topic of conversation was politics. (Ann kept detailed notes on everyone she met in her address book.) It was almost certainly this trip which pushed Ann towards journalism.

At one time she had toyed with the idea of modelling, sufficiently seriously to undergo private surgery to alter the shape of her nose. Her passport picture, the one which appeared on the front page of the Athens newspapers, does not look like her at all. The slightly protruding nose had been replaced by a shortened, flared version which transformed her appearance and gave her deep smile a fresh new significance. A boyfriend, one of the few, took attractive pictures of her by the river Thames. Tragically, far from launching her career as a model, these pictures were reproduced in newspapers and magazines only after her death.

Despite her travels, Ann remained close to her family, although feeling a little unconnected with their traditional, rather homespun, world. Her room in the family home at Putney was stacked with books and mementos of her travels. Edward Chapman recalls that she went out a lot but rarely stayed away from home at night. There were no close boy-friends. 'She was what I would call "normal" about boys,' he told me. 'She was always more interested in her career, trying to get into the BBC and meeting the right people who could help her.' Whether she always met the 'right' people at the Troubadour is questionable, but it is clear that the drive to get on and make something of herself powered Ann to an overwhelming extent. She was also increasingly feeling that life with her parents was restricting, because early in 1971, in the last year of her life, she was thinking about moving to share a flat with her old schoolfriend, Danny Lessing. The Chapmans now remember the episode with some resentment, because they think it took Ann away from them at a crucial time. Danny visited the Chapman home in Putney often and soon started to ring up regularly, encouraging Ann to move out. Dorothy Chapman was much disquieted to hear news of this plan not from Ann but from Danny, who told her on the telephone that the pair of them were already looking for a flat. This sudden disclosure made up Ann's mind. A flat was found in Cathcart Road, in Earl's Court, comfortably close to the Troubadour. In July 1971, she moved in while her parents were on holiday in Spain, where they heard the news with dismay. It was one of the few occasions when Ann indulged in mild deceit of her parents. Dorothy Chapman was greatly upset and blames Danny Lessing for putting pressure on Ann. Yet the family relationship survived. Ann took her mother out to lunch regularly and she came home to Putney often.

The move to Cathcart Road was not a great success. Danny's job as a busy young house doctor working long hours meant that Ann was often alone, if she was not at the Troubadour. She hinted to her mother that she was unhappy about this. And there was a degree of friction between Ann and Danny over Gareth Davis who had been seeing Danny before meeting Ann at Cathcart Road. Davis seems to have dropped Danny immediately – though he says now that the relationship with her 'never really started' – to chase Ann.

Following Michael Vestey's introduction, Ann started work at Radio London early in February 1971, six months before she moved out of her parents' home. She was quickly off on a round of 'soft' stories which ended up as snippets in magazine programmes for housebound women and rush-hour motorists. It is clear that she found real satisfaction hunting for stories, dashing all over London with her tape-recorder. Her diary contains a good record of the material she produced: the Miss London contest, a women's liberation demo, the gypsy education council, on one occasion a trip to Wormwood Scrubs prison. Ann was trying hard to make her mark, researching her own stories and pushing vigorously to get them on the air. This was a typical entry, for 28 August 1971: 'Derek Guyler 2.30 – try the morning show?'

Ann flew in and out so much that hardly anyone at the station had the opportunity to get close to her. Within nine months she had arranged the trip to Greece. Like most others at the station, the Rev. Blennerhassett was surprised: 'There was a gut feeling that she was not sufficiently experienced.' Everyone knew that Ann was looking for a better story than tourism but no one appears to have warned her clearly that she was too inexperienced for such a risky venture and that it could be dangerous. The Rev. Blennerhassett clearly recalls that she was determined 'to get something else out of this trip', the big story. And a few hours before boarding her flight to Greece she told her mother, 'I have a big story which is going to make my name for me.'

2 · The Elephant and the Flea

What is or is not Greece, is a question of no little difficulty.

—Murray's *Encyclopaedia of Geography*, 1834

Since Greece's bloody liberation from Turkey more than a century and a half ago, chronic instability and the failure to construct enduring political structures have resulted in a national drama in which the country reels between plots, revolutions, dictatorships, constitutional upheavals and civil wars. The former president, Constantine Karamanlis, who succeeded the Colonels and who was himself deposed, has lamented the failure of his countrymen to evolve 'a calm political atmosphere and calm political habits and customs'. Despite or even because of the dangerous and uncertain political climate, the Greeks have been obsessed by the intoxicating notion of the 'Great Idea', the rebirth of an Hellenic Empire with Constantinople as its capital. The most famous Greek nationalist and Hellenic expansionist Eleutherios Venizelos came deceptively close to realizing the dream before his death in 1936. Venizelos used guile, gunpowder and statecraft to expand dramatically the national territory of the weakling nation which had been ushered into life by the great powers of Europe in 1827.

The origins of what we now call Greece lie in such distant times that no modern searchlight can distinguish history from mythology. Given its enormous and yet indefinable

21

inheritance, the fledgling Greek state was unlikely to be satisfied by the modest boundaries conceded at the end of its long and bitter struggle to free itself from Turkish domination. This obsession with the Great Idea played its part in luring the Colonels to their fatal destiny in Cyprus in 1974. 'Enosis', the union of Greece and Cyprus, always seemed potentially the brightest jewel in the Hellenic crown. Yet, as the present Greek premier, Andreas Papandreou, pointedly observed while prudently sheltering abroad from the junta: 'Cyprus lies at the heart of the tragic political developments that have led to the death of democracy in Greece.'

The Greeks also suffer from an excess of self-importance which men like Karamanlis always fought to subdue; namely, the belief that Greece lies at the centre of the world's political interest, 'the navel of the earth'. Karamanlis liked to tell the story that when archaeologists working at Delphi reported they had discovered the stone which the ancients believed to be that very navel, he urged them to cast it into the sea immediately. Almost everything that Karamanlis did after the Colonels fell from power can be framed as the political equivalent of his advice to the archaeologists at Delphi (with the significant exception of his refusal to 'open the Cyprus file' and reveal the true fate of Ann Chapman). The new realism which Karamanlis tried to project is dramatically illustrated by the gamble he took in virtually throwing Greece into the European Community in 1982. It was an attempt to weld the country once and for all into the military and economic geo-system of the Western alliance, in the face of what has always been another abiding distraction for the Greeks – the conviction that they are constantly abused by foreign interests and intervention. This stems from the fact that, whatever Greeks like to think or are encouraged to believe today, their independence and sovereignty was assured in the first place by external forces. Despite the internal insurrection against the Turks, it was the treaty signed in

London in 1827 which guaranteed an independent Greece, and even after that it was still necessary for a combined British, Russian and French fleet to annihilate the Ottoman navy at the Battle of Navarino later that year. The Greeks try to obfuscate all this by celebrating their independence day on 25 March, dating from 1821, the first popular revolt against Turkish dominion, instead of selecting 1827, or even 1832 when the young Bavarian prince, Otho, accepted the crown.

Of course, it is true that Greece's strategic location renders it irresistibly attractive to greater powers, regionally and globally. It represents the balcony of Europe, looking out over clear views of the communist-controlled Balkans and the waters which lap the fratricidal states of the Middle East. An anchorage astride the vital sea-route to the Suez Canal makes Greece crucial to the southern flanks of NATO's security arrangements. American bases in Greece monitor and deter Soviet expansion in the eastern Mediterranean, although Hellenic xenophobia is fuelled by a belief, expertly articulated by contemporary politicians such as Andreas Papandreou, that they are actually a launch-pad for intrigue inside Greece itself. What is certainly correct is that succeeding US administrations, deeply concerned by the cold war between Greece and Turkey and eager for a settlement to the Cyprus question, have indeed manipulated the navigation and direction of the Greek state.

Christopher Hitchens suggested in 1985: 'Cyprus was to American foreign policy the counterpart, in timing and character, of Watergate in domestic policy.' The reference to Watergate is apt, because the House Select Committee on Intelligence discovered after the fall of the junta that CIA funds used to run the Greek intelligence service had been partially recycled to finance Richard Nixon's re-election campaign. The committee, which had launched a probe into the extent of US involvement in the Cyprus affair, discovered a web of entanglement spreading out from the American embassy and CIA station in Athens. Henry Tasca, Nixon's ambassador to Greece, directed a policy of official nourishment of the junta and was deeply implicated in the plot by which one dictator, the 'first colonel', George Papadopoulos, was eclipsed by a second, Dimitrios Ioannides. Tasca had seen to it that the Greek intelligence agency, the KYP, jumped to strings pulled by the CIA.

In 1979 Henry Tasca was killed in a car smash in Switzerland. There have been strong hints of revenge-taking in the wake of the junta's collapse, and even the sober historian C. M. Woodhouse, who usually resists a conspiratorial view of the CIA's role in the dictatorship, concedes that few in Greece today are prepared to regard Tasca's death as purely accidental.

It had long been the aim of American foreign policy to secure a 'final solution' to the problem of Cyprus. In 1964, when serious inter-communal fighting broke out between Turks and Greeks on the island and threatened to spark war between Turkey and Greece, President Lyndon Johnson urgently despatched the former Secretary of State Dean Acheson on a crisis mission. From that mission emerged what became known as the 'Acheson plan', the essential points of which proposed a Turkish-dominated canton in the north, with the rest of the island ceded to Greece. Johnson was haunted by a vision of Cyprus as the 'Cuba of the Mediterranean'. He reckoned that by appeasing both Greece and Turkey over their unresolved territorial claims on the island, he could neutralize a quarrel which threatened to split NATO and wreck American strategy in the region, not to mention handing the Soviet Union a most attractive fire-cracker. But the Greek government at the time, headed by George Papandreou (whose son is now Prime Minister), was not in a compliant mood. He told Johnson bluntly during a visit to Washington that the Greek people could not possibly accept such a plan. The President exploded with anger. He tried to blackmail Papandreou by threatening to cut off all NATO aid to Greece. Papandreou replied that in those circumstances he might pre-empt the threat by pulling Greece out of NATO. He patiently tried to explain to Johnson that he would never get the Acheson plan past the Greek Parliament, to which Johnson imperiously riposted, 'Maybe Greece should rethink the value of a parliament which could not take the right decision.' In view of subsequent US involvement in the Colonels' coup, this was a dangerously prophetic remark. Johnson's rage over what he saw as Greek intransigence over a Cyprus solution did not subside. A few days later, he made this remarkable outburst to the Greek ambassador in Washington, Alexander Matsas:

Fuck your parliament and your constitution. America is an elephant. Cyprus is a flea. If these two fellows continue itching the elephant, they may just get whacked by the elephant's trunk, whacked good. If your Prime Minister gives me talk about democracy, parliament and consti-tution, he, his parliament and his constitution may not last very long.

And indeed they did not. Within three years of Johnson's incandescent lecture to the Greek ambassador, democracy, Parliament and democratic constitution in Greece had all perished. The first moves towards realizing the Acheson plan lay only two years away. The young and inexperienced Greek monarch, Constantine, had long been falling under the influ-ence of the CIA, who regarded him as a pliant agent for the fulfilment of secret American objectives in Cyprus. The Americans installed their own minder close to the throne, one Colonel Lipczyk, who followed the King everywhere, even to Malta for a bizarre six-day holiday playing squash (about which Constantine was fanatical), just before the Colonels' coup. The account of this strange interlude comes from Martin Packard, an enigmatic 'Greenmantle' figure who, despite being a serving British naval officer, later became a significant participant in the resistance to the junta (see Chapter 3). Packard was married to the daughter of a Greek MP and became friendly with Constantine on the squash courts during social visits to Athens. He made all the arrangements for the visit to Malta. The British authorities were infuriated by Packard's buccaneering initiative, especially when Constantine insisted on bringing the ubiquitous Colonel Lipczyk to an official dinner. Packard was told bluntly by the Commander-in-Chief in Malta, Admiral Sir John Hamilton: 'We are not having those bloody Americans here.' But Lipczyk received his invitation after Constantine had warned Packard privately: 'If he doesn't come, there will be extremely serious consequences for Greece.'

This episode is important only because it underlines the extent of Constantine's subservience to the CIA, just months after, at their behest, he had ousted his own premier, George Papandreou. A crucial element in Papandreou's fall was the so-called 'Aspida' affair. The word, which means 'shield' in Greek, was alleged to be the code-name of a secret organization of radical young army officers. A huge political row broke out when Papandreou's son, Andreas, then a minister in his father's government, was accused of links with Aspida. An inquiry was launched by the Minister of Defence, Petros Garouphalias, a close intimate of the King, whom the elder Papandreou suspected of blocking his plans to install army officers loyal to his shaky government. Papandreou was momentarily caught off-balance and offered his resignation to the King in the belief that Constantine would either back down or call an election. Acting on CIA advice, the King did neither but instead installed another Prime Minister of his own choosing. The move was entirely unconstitutional but now Constantine had unleashed forces he could not control.

His first choice as premier did not survive a vote of confidence in Parliament, but the second, Stephanos Stephanopoulos, held the job until the Colonels seized power. Stephanopoulos began to make a number of key appointments, thus installing, with the King's unwitting approval, the plotters who would ensure his downfall and the end of democracy in Greece. In came Grigorios Spandidakis as Chief of the General Staff, later to be jailed as a junta conspirator. From a remote command in Thrace the key conspirator, Colonel George Papadopoulos, was summoned to Athens to sit on the General Staff in the building which is named, like its American equivalent, the Pentagon. Nicos Makarezos and Spelios Pattakos, who would receive death sentences for high treason in 1975, were also given important posts at the centre of power.

Colonel George Papadopoulos had been on the payroll of the CIA since the early 1950s, acting as a link between Greek intelligence and their American masters. Another conspirator with whom the Americans had consorted was Brigadier Dimitrios Ioannides, a sadist with the mind of an unreconstructed Nazi. As head of the Greek military police, ESA, he would unleash a regime of dungeon torture. Many of the victims were taken to the ESA headquarters, located directly opposite the American embassy from which no protests emerged, despite the well-documented evidence of brutal ill-treatment set before the Council of Europe in Strasburg in 1969–70.

Ioannides was important to the Americans because of his uncompromising attitude to their plans for a solution in Cyprus. He believed in Enosis, pure and simple, and any means of getting it would suit him. His past links with Colonel George Grivas, founder of the EOKA (union with Greece) movement which fought a long campaign against the British, had bequeathed an association with a highly unscrupulous figure called Nikos Sampson. In 1964, during the inter-communal riots then raging across the island, Ioannides, together with Sampson, turned up for a secret meeting with

27

the Cypriot Head of State, Archbishop Makarios, the man whom Lyndon Johnson feared might become a 'clerical Castro'. Years later, Makarios revealed the astonishing proposal which Ioannides and Sampson had brought with them. They prescribed instant Enosis by ridding the island of every Turkish Cypriot man, woman and child in a programme of mass genocide. A genuinely shocked Makarios sent this grim pair packing but the idea nevertheless remained lurking in Ioannides' deranged mind. In 1973 the Americans would install this psychopath as dictator of Greece and he, in turn, would despatch to Cyprus his angel of death, Nikos Sampson, with orders to wipe out the Turkish Cypriots and bring back the head of Makarios. With ESA, the instrument which he had fashioned into a Greek gestapo, he enjoyed the perfect facility to deal with awkward people who might threaten these schemes, like Ann Chapman.

By 1967, that situation which Greece had so often faced before and which Karamanlis described as 'incurable political incompetence' brought the country to the edge of chaos. The fall of George Papandreou left a political vacuum which Constantine struggled to fill. Rumours of an impending coup were flying all over the capital and of course they were true, because Papadopoulos and his friends had by now made virtually all their plans with the connivance of the United States. The CIA believed that Constantine had lost control and should now be regarded as expendable. The King found himself propelled towards the election he had struggled to avoid. American fears concentrated on a victory for the Left, which would certainly loosen their control of Greece, and interrupt their plans for the long-desired solution in Cyprus. There was a clumsy attempt to link the King's name with the plot now being prepared which he, to his credit, toughly rejected, declaring: 'Do you imagine I don't know that *any* dictatorship would be certain to get rid of me?' George Papandreou remained deeply preoccupied with the extremist sentiments of his son, Andreas, who was still under suspicion in the 'Aspida' secret officers' guild affair. In surprising concert with the Americans, the ex-premier became convinced that unless the situation was arrested quickly, there might be a dangerous drift towards instability and then communism. The old political sage could clearly detect the whiff of revolution in the air. He retained sufficient of his powers to engineer the collapse of the government and the King was compelled, at last, to agree to a general election. May 27th was selected as the date. The Greek people, by now thoroughly unnerved by the unfolding crisis, looked for a strong government to lead them out of the muddle, a national mood later tapped with considerable success by the Colonels. In marked contrast, George Papandreou viewed himself as the only potential saviour, an idea which thoroughly alarmed the CIA. Papandreou, *père et fils*, had also confused absolutely everything by plunging into a public slanging match. Andreas had become highly volatile, lashing out not only at his father, whom he believed to be making political deals behind his back, but also at the palace and the Americans for good measure as well. He was also fighting to avoid being dragged into the courts on charges connected with Aspida once his parliamentary immunity was automatically suspended during the election period.

While preparation for that election on 27 May ground slowly forward, others were doing their own intensive homework. The game had almost been given away a few months before, when preparations for a 'Greek military putsch', to be sponsored by the CIA and the Defense Department in Washington, were intercepted by two visiting American VIPs. Their subsequent confidential memorandum was promptly fed into the political shredder by a furious Lyndon Johnson. In Athens, the CIA kept the King in ignorance of what was about to happen, fearful that he would finally summon up the traditional loyalists in the navy to frustrate Papadopoulos and the plotters inside the Greek Pentagon – and the American one as well. All the major figures in the revolutionary group met at the home of Pattakos on 18 April and decided against any further delay. At precisely 2 a.m. on the morning of 21 April, tanks and soldiers moved on to the streets of Athens. Using the standard coup practice, the telephone exchange and radio station were first seized, while prominent politicians and loyal officers were rounded up and imprisoned or placed under house arrest.

Greece woke up to military rule. The elephant's trunk had finally struck the Greek flea.

3 · All the King's Men

We few, we happy few, we band of brothers
—William Shakespeare, *Henry V*

Because the Colonels had moved with deadly precision, there was no opportunity to organize resistance. The King, woken from his bed in the middle of the night, was allowed to wear the uniform of a field marshal and to talk to members of the former government who were now just as helpless as he. The baton of power was grasped firmly by the triumvirate at the Pentagon – Papadopoulos, Pattakos and Makarezos. At the American embassy the ambassador, Phillips Talbot, protested weakly about being 'taken by surprise' which was, of course, absurd, given the nocturnal fraternization between the CIA and the plotters. Five thousand miles away across the Atlantic, Lyndon Johnson received with quiet satisfaction the news of a virtually bloodless 'Greek military putsch'. Helen Vlachos, editor of the influential newspaper *Kathimerini*, eventually managed to get through to the bewildered Constantine on the telephone. 'I am completely isolated, completely alone,' he told her. The CIA had cynically transported their attentions elsewhere. Journalists, particularly those representing foreign newspapers, were allowed to see the important detainees like Andreas Papandreou but others, especially communists, were held incommunicado; some were beaten, even murdered, away from prying foreign eyes. The crushing weight of censorship was imposed on the country and within a short time Helen Vlachos was forced to take her newspaper off the streets.

Such resistance as there was proved sporadic and ineffective. A small group which took its inspiration from Andreas Papandreou was promptly identified and the core of its membership given long gaol sentences. A Patriotic Anti-Dictatorship Front sprang up towards the end of May, and in August the first was heard of Democratic Defence, most of whose supporters were drawn from the old Centre Union party which, like all others, had disappeared in the complete ban on political activity. There were sporadic bombings but these, perversely, served the junta's interest because they gave credence to the claim that the country was at risk from destabilizing forces. The Colonels basked in a warm climate of tolerance, winning political recognition almost immediately from most of the major powers, including the Soviet Union. But an iron fist continued to strike at every sign of subversion. In November, the popular song-writer Theodorakis was imprisoned for supporting the Anti-Dictatorship Front. He was thus assured of instant political martyrdom since his music continued to inspire every Greek who understood that whatever the Colonels pretended about their motives for seizing power their basic philosophy amounted to no more than a vision of Greece as one enormous parade ground.

It quickly became obvious that genuine opposition to the regime would have to be fermented outside Greece. Helen Vlachos reached that conclusion in December and decided to escape from house arrest and flee to London. She looked first to the American embassy for help, only to receive a firm cold-shoulder from Phillips Talbot. 'Why don't you try a smaller embassy, Helen?' Mrs Vlachos, who is now in her seventies and firmly back in command of her newspaper in Athens, told me in 1985 that she had never thought of herself at the time as a dangerous revolutionary. She was not quite sure where to look for help but grateful that if no one was actually prepared to do much to facilitate her escape, at least she was not betrayed. The underground network which would subsequently organize escapes did not then exist. So in a fine freelance effort, she borrowed papers from her sister-in-law – 'who does not look a bit like me' – and scampered over the rooftop of her flat to escape the six guards posted at the front door. She made her way to Thessalonika and flew on to Vienna and London, where the story of her escape caused a mild sensation. Hundreds of journalists turned up for an impromptu press conference at the Grosvenor Hotel. She soon joined a small group of exiles who drew comfort from each other and used key figures in the liberal establishment, like Sir Hugh Greene, in an effort to excite British public opinion about the situation in Greece. But British public opinion was already yawning. The Labour government, headed by Harold Wilson, had already recognized the military junta and wanted no political boat-rocking. The reasons for socialist co-existence with a quasi-fascist regime were to be understood only much later. Helen Vlachos continued to be a star performer in the media as the 'Free Voice of Greece' but interest in the fate of the country was quickly waning. A group of Greek exiles and British Hellenophiles adopted the approach of forming a London Committee Against the Greek Dictatorship. The first meeting was held in the flat of the economist George Yannopoulos, a lecturer at Reading University. He remembers today that the committee was primarily a public relations exercise designed to stimulate political opposition to the regime, but even at this early stage many potential activists were convinced that being polite, even to each other, was a waste of time.

The first signs of serious fissures inside the resistance were soon apparent. Some of those became major political earthquakes, the after-shocks of which still raise dust in Greece today. The resistance movement grew three heads: the communists, as always, ran their own show; the remaining leftist elements had their sights set on power in the post-junta future and for that reason grouped rapidly around Andreas Papandreou; and Democratic Defence became the umbrella for the old centrists and moderate conservatives who were handicapped by the lack of a charismatic leader. Karamanlis, their natural choice, was brooding loftily in a flat in Paris and infinitely preferred the role of statesman-in-exile. It is not surprising, therefore, that Papandreou – once the Colonels had freed him from prison – seized the opportunity to commence his bid for power.

In mid-January 1968 Papandreou flew to Paris where he made excitable statements about some kind of 'guerrilla warfare' being required to defeat the Colonels. These were strange sentiments from a man who had spent the whole of World War II and the subsequent civil war safely away from the gunfire in the peaceful security of the United States. Destabilizing ideas exercised a curious fascination for Papandreou throughout his years in exile. George Yannopoulos recalls one encounter with him at a hotel in Wiesbaden, West Germany, where a conference of all the resistance leaders in Europe had been summoned at Christmas 1970. It was a gloomy affair from the start because, on all the evidence before them, absolutely nothing the resistance had done so far appeared to have budged the Colonels' hold on Greece by one centimetre. On the contrary, they looked more secure than ever. One of Papandreou's principal aides, Gregoris Stathis – who is now a socialist MP – sketched the problem simply: 'The main difficulty is that there is no opposition to the regime. For that reason we cannot collect money in the States because people there think the Greeks are not sufficiently dissatisfied with the regime. Therefore, we think that something more spectacular is required to indicate there is real, serious opposition.' Stathis, says Yannopoulos, then stunned everyone in the room: 'I think the best way is a political assassination –

it doesn't matter who it is.' They all looked at Andreas Papandreou to see how he would react to this cold-blooded talk about killing. Yannopoulos remembers: 'I could see him at the centre of the table, smoking his pipe, totally expressionless. Low spirits dropped even further. 'We were all shocked,' says Yannopoulos.

Papandreou left Paris for Stockholm, where he established the headquarters of the embryonic Pan-Hellenic Liberation Movement (PAK), which he would later transform into the socialist party, PASOK, which rules Greece today. Among the early visitors to the PAK headquarters was a young Norwegian journalist Arne Treholdt, who offered his services, eagerly accepted, as an adviser. Thereafter Treholdt had an open channel on everything the resistance was doing. This connection was later to cause Papandreou acute discomfort. In 1984 Treholdt, having meanwhile climbed to high pinnacles in the Norwegian state, was unmasked as a Russian spy and later jailed for twenty years although no one, including Papandreou, had an inkling at the time that a Soviet mole had burrowed into their organization.

Papandreou's overbearing ambitions meanwhile began to set up strains everywhere. In London he antagonized Yannopoulos by indulging in the pretence that he was mobilizing opposition on behalf of his father's old party, the Centre Union, which was not true. The friendship broke as Papandreou's real hopes for PAK, and himself, emerged. There were tensions in Paris, too. A key worker there was George Lianopoulis, a gentle and mild-mannered traditional centrist later to hold Cabinet office in the first post-junta Karamanlis government. The Paris front was very shaky with, as Lianopoulis told me, 'much discussion and quarrelling with no point or purpose, that being the nature of Greeks'. Papandreou had been making ferocious attacks on the Americans and the British, which Lianopoulis conceived to be wholly counterproductive and certain to delay the day of liberation.

His friendship with Papandreou was dead by the summer of 1969. It was frequently observed that when he visited Paris, Papandreou grew moody and anxious, almost certainly because he resented the presence there of Karamanlis, whom the world seemed to prefer as the voice of free Greece and the best hope for the restoration of democracy. Resistance workers recall a dinner in the French capital when an obviously overwrought Papandreou sprang to his feet and suddenly declaimed loudly: 'God sent *me* to save Greece.' His American wife Margaret calmed him down. In August 1968, Papandreou's fears seemed justified when an influential group of exiles called for a union of opposition forces headed by Karamanlis, who coolly dismissed the notion – and his rival. 'One and one do not always make two, they sometimes make zero.' Sixteen years later, Andreas Papandreou would enjoy a sweet revenge for that remark.

The floundering resistance movement had meanwhile begun to attract the attention of independent spirits. One of these was Martin Packard, the serving British naval officer based with intelligence staff in Malta, who had joined the service as a boy cadet at the end of the war in 1945 and proved such promising material that he moved quickly up through the ranks first as Midshipman, then as Sub-Lieutenant, before qualifying as a pilot in 1954. When the storm broke over Greece and Cyprus, Packard had already acquired strong Greek connections through his wife's family and leisure hours spent with Constantine on the squash courts. In the early days of the Cyprus troubles, Packard had been detached from naval staff, first to act as an interpreter between the two communities because he spoke Greek, and then as a UN peacemaker. He was awarded the MBE in the 1964 honours list for duties which the London *Gazette* records 'required tact and courage'. Peter Preston, now editor of the *Guardian*, was then a correspondent on the island and remembers Packard as a flamboyant, colourful character, quite capable of defusing dramatic tensions between Greek and Turkish Cypriots as well as being an unpredictable 'T. E. Lawrence figure'. His flamboyance earned him enemies. In 1964, Major-General Michael Carver, then deputy chief of the UN forces in Cyprus, ordered the return of Lieutenant Commander Martin Packard and his deputy, Major John Burgess, to their own units because, according to an official despatch, 'it was inadvisable that British officers should carry out liaison duties involving contacts with both sides'. Packard recalls: 'I was flown out to Athens as if I had the plague. I was deeply shocked.' He is convinced that his undoing lay in the plan he had evolved to re-integrate the two Cypriot communities, starting with a handful of villages in June 1964. The plan was unscrambled as soon as he left, proof, believes Packard, of British connivance with American support to sabotage anything which even smelt of an integrated Cyprus. As the situation deteriorated, the Turkish Cypriots began demanding partition and attitudes were further hardened by the arrival from Athens of Colonel George Grivas, the former EOKA guerrilla commander, to lead the Cyprus National Guard.

After a sojourn in Athens Packard rejoined naval intelligence in Malta, where he became convinced that the CIA were planning a coup in Cyprus and furthermore the British knew all about it. The UN establishment meanwhile had not forgotten their admiration for Packard and persuaded the navy to second him to them indefinitely. In preparation he spent a year at Durham University, learning Arabic. On the eve of the coup, Packard was spending a few weeks on holiday in Athens with his wife, which offered him the opportunity to see the King and tell him about his premonition that something was about to happen. Returning to London to report these fears to the Foreign Office, Packard was firmly told that this kind of intelligence was totally at variance with 'official reports'. Within days *Evening Standard* placards were

37

shouting: 'King's men seize power.' But all the King's men were either under arrest or powerless to stop Papadopoulos. Packard rushed back to Greece, knowing that his wife and her family would fight the junta. Still a serving officer, fresh from a job on intelligence staff, Packard began to behave provocatively right under the noses of his naval bosses and would continue to do so. He was introduced to the founder of Democratic Defence, Vassili Filias, a professor at Athens University who feared arrest at any moment. Packard hit on the ploy of providing him with cover as a private language instructor while giving the infant resistance movement advice on how to organize basic moves like secret codes and passing messages. As pressure mounted on Filias, Packard provided a safe home in his flat. Filias' memories of all this remain firmly affectionate. 'Martin was one of the best, he never let us down,' he told me.

Packard's strange career continued. He remained a naval officer, while conspiring against a government which Britain recognized. A cynical mind could observe that he was in the ideal position to play the intelligence game both ways; but Filias, who owed so much to him, completely rejects any notion of treachery. However, Asteris Stagos, a journalist who fled the Colonels to help set up the resistance base in London, was more than suspicious. He wrote to Filias warning that Packard was betraying them. In 1985, elderly and ill with heart trouble, Stagos told me in his tiny Athens flat: 'I suspected Packard from the first moment. There were others I didn't trust too, mostly collaborators of Packard.' He claimed that many of the items sent to Greece by the Packard network, such as explosives, arrived damaged or destroyed.

Spyros Mercouris – brother of the actress-turned-politician, Melina – was reluctant to talk about Packard when I met him at his Athens office in February 1985. Mercouris denied that Packard had ever been closely connected with Democratic Defence – despite his friendship with its founder, Filias – but conceded that the 'stories were conflicting' and he would like to see the truth emerge. Coming down in the lift after our meeting, I asked Mercouris what impression he gained from Martin Packard when they met. He replied: 'I only met him once. I said – thank you very much for all you have done. Please do not do any more.' In January 1983, a series of sensational articles appeared in the Greek newspaper *Eleftherotypia*, written by Yannis Andricopoulos, a freelance contributor working from London. The substance of his reports was that Packard headed his own network inside the resistance movement, 'Group C', which, Andricopoulos claimed, was no more than a cover for penetration by British intelligence services. Andricopoulos also suggested that some of the extraordinary characters who featured in the Packard network had talked to Ann Chapman before she left for Greece. It can certainly be established that Ann did know some of these people – her former boss Professor Northedge was in touch with some of the key figures like John Dragoumis; she may have met others at the Troubadour coffee bar, and possibly made one contact while working at the Berlitz language school in Paris in 1968. But Andricopoulos also went on to allege that Mercouris was sent to Europe to close down the Packard network because of suspicions about his real motives. Our conversation in the lift in Athens does not suggest any warmth between the two men, and nor did Mercouris trouble to deny that he told Packard immediately to end his work for the resistance. When I talked to Packard in London in the summer of 1985, he supplied an intriguing alternative explanation. Filias and Andreas Papandreou had begun the campaign of resistance as close friends, having worked together in a radical political discussion club in Athens. But as the long years of the junta wore on, they became estranged, as happened in many other Papandreou friendships. Packard thought an element of this might have been a belief – sustained by the CIA defector Philip Agee –

that there had been 'a long-standing relationship' between Papandreou and American intelligence. As Filias, the close friend of Packard, moved away from the Papandreou faction, Spyros Mercouris moved closer, to the point where he now has a senior job in his sister Melina's Ministry of Culture. By the summer of 1985, Filias had turned completely against Andreas Papandreou. At the funeral of a resistance member, Professor Karageorges, who had never fully recovered from injuries inflicted when a home-made bomb exploded prematurely, Filias delivered a long oration which amounted to a virtual condemnation of Papandreou and everything he stood for. He told me: 'Papandreou tried to trap Democratic Defence inside PASOK. He expelled members of Democratic Defence for no reason whatsoever. He thought we were plotting against him, but he was plotting also.' If Packard was among those expellees, as Mercouris seems to confirm, then it is more than plausible that it was all part of Papandreou's ambition to fashion the Pan-Hellenic Resistance Movement into his personal instrument of power and future government. Should Packard pose any threat to those objectives he, like others, would have to go. Small wonder Packard now bitterly condemns the role of Papandreou in the restoration of Greek democracy.

In the Athens of early 1968, these contortions were yet to come. Not surprisingly, Martin Packard had taxed the patience of his British naval masters too far. He declares that he was suddenly arrested, put under military orders and despatched straight back to London – 'We know everything you have been up to' – and warned that he faced court martial. In his pocket was a list of people Vassili Filias wanted him to contact in London: George Yannopoulos, George Koutsoumbas – a convenient 'sleeper' at Olympic Airways – and Stagos, who would later accuse him of betrayal. In the event, Packard did not appear before a court martial, but says that instead he was given three months to pack his bags and leave the navy after a career lasting twenty-five years. The navy list for the year shows him posted to HMS *Warrior*, the naval communications centre at Northwood. So far as the Naval Secretary is concerned, he left the service 'at his own request' on 24 August 1968, although his official departure seems not to have been officially gazetted until two years later, in 1970. In April 1986, he wrote to me: 'Since I left the Navy in 1968, I have not seen any official documents – and I have no idea when my retirement was gazetted. For that, and such other anomalies as may surface, I would assume that some logical explanation does exist: but at this long distance, it may be hard to identify.' So Packard was firmly of the impression that he was a free agent when he flew back to Greece, travelling on a borrowed passport, to deal with the sudden crisis which erupted when the senior Democratic Defence man in the country, Filias, was finally caught in a swoop by the junta's police. Packard says it was this event which prompted him to throw everything into the resistance movement, including £10,000 of his own money. Like others, Packard became convinced that the revolt had to be manipulated from outside Greece. Back in London again, he was soon working furiously to patch together a group of adventurers who would launch Boy's-Own-paper-type raids on the country, delivering subversive material.

At Durham University, Packard had played squash with a young Swede, Kit Zweigbrek, who was deeply and intellectually opposed to the 1967 coup. They met up again in 1968 and hatched thrilling plans to sail to Greece to rescue opponents of the regime. Packard's house in north Oxford was the scene of a clandestine meeting to plan the expedition. Those present apart from Packard included Roger Williams, a young journalist who had gone to school with Zweigbrek, and John Dragoumis. Roger Williams recalls that the sailing boat expedition quickly fell through but he decided nevertheless to do all he could to support the group. Regular transport to

Greece was the key. A link was set up to a wealthy young racing driver, Peter Johnson, who ran a garage in Oxford. Cars were taken there for technical surgery, at the hands of Johnson's friend, Michael Hudson. George Forrest, a sympathetic academic in Oxford, ran a secret bank account to cover the operations and acted as Packard's link man with the operations at Johnson's garage. Packard would ring up Forrest and ask simply 'Is the car ready?' Roger Williams became a senior courier on the long overland treks to Greece for almost eighteen months, well into 1969, posing as a tourist at the Greek frontier. 'We were all frankly a bunch of amateurs,' he says now, 'and a lot of times I thought I should stop but somehow it seemed difficult to get out of, once the commitment had been made.' Mostly Williams trafficked in two-way radios, passports for people who wanted to get out of the country and occasionally consignments of explosives. Michael Hudson once delivered two false passports for Lady Amelia Fleming, but that operation went wrong when the hand-over contacts failed to turn up at the secret rendezvous.

The explosives were prepared by Greeks in Britain – primitive devices consisting of simple concoctions of weedkiller or fertilizer and a basic timing device, all packed into a wooden box. Michael Hudson devised ingenious methods of concealment under seats and behind panelling. Stagos was later to claim that many of the bombs were duds but Williams recalls testing one together with a resistance member on a highway north of Athens: 'It went off with one hell of a bang and frightened me half to death.' The explosives which did reach the hands of the resistance were usually no more than an irritant to the Colonels and the flimsy organization of the resistance structure inside Greece rarely gave them the opportunity to strike hard at military targets. The most dramatic incident occurred on 13 August 1968, when the junta leader, Papadopoulos, was travelling in armed convoy along the coastal road from his home towards Athens. A powerful

charge exploded in a culvert beneath the road, and Papadopoulos narrowly escaped assassination. A young army de-
serter, Alexander Panagoulis, who had been hiding with
Democratic Defence friends, was arrested and, after being
horribly tortured, sentenced to death. Whether Panagoulis
had received the explosives from the Packard chain will never
be clear. He denied receiving help from accomplices although
the resistance headquarters in Paris swiftly claimed full
knowledge and responsibility for the attack. The Colonels
were clearly more than disturbed by the revelation that, after
going underground in Athens, Panagoulis had managed to
reach Cyprus furtively with, it is known, the aid of Makarios.
He was thus seen as an agent with sinister motives which lay
far beyond the removal of Papadopoulos from the scene. (In
1976, Panagoulis, who had been reprieved from the death
sentence, died in a car crash. On the morning of his death he
had tried desperately to contact Vassili Filias, who was
stunned to hear news of the fatal crash later in the day on the
radio. Panagoulis had said to Filias' secretary that he needed
to see him urgently. There are many in Greece today who
believe that, like Ambassador Tasca, Panagoulis lost his life
in revenge.)

In 1969 the career of Roger Williams, resistance agent and
courier, came to an abrupt end. He had driven to the eastern
docks at Dover in a Porsche borrowed from a friend who
was serving with British forces on the Rhine. The Porsche,
carrying BAOR plates, was swooped upon by Special Branch
officers. The London evening papers, carrying news of the
incident and Williams' arrest, said there were enough explosives aboard to blow up 'half the docks'. Recalling the incident
seventeen years later, Williams was amused by the thought
that a cargo of home-made fertilizer bombs might have devas-
tated Dover. Special Branch gave him a thorough interrogation, concentrating on links with Martin Packard. 'They
knew all about him,' Williams told me. Who tipped off the

police before the Porsche arrived at Dover remains a mystery. But Packard's cover had already been revealed, Williams thinks, by a couple living in south London who were friends of the exiled journalist Asteris Stagos. Williams, who had every reason to believe he was in deep trouble, received a surprisingly light sentence – a fine of just £50. This was because the magistrate ruled that the original charge of possessing explosives for an unlawful purpose – which could send him to gaol for fourteen years – was technically invalid on the grounds that the 'unlawful purpose' could not be decided by an English court. Williams and Michael Hudson immediately pulled out of the resistance movement. 'We realized we had lost our effectiveness and that we were under surveillance by the police. And after nearly two years, I had had enough – it was a good "out" for me.' In the wake of the Dover incident, Packard's home was raided – the first of many occasions, he claims – by the police.

The breaking of Packard's cover by the Special Branch and, through them, by MI5, posed severe problems for the integrity of the network he had created and, more significantly, for the Oxford garage operation. The police now knew the names of many people who had been working with Packard, including that of Peter Johnson. He was in his garage when detectives arrived without warning, searching for a car. They asked many questions about Packard and gave the place a thorough search, without a warrant. They found no explosives, only a few grammes of cannabis in a plastic bag. Roger Williams says Johnson was told that the drugs would be 'overlooked' if he agreed to implicate Williams and Packard in a conspiracy to export explosives. Johnson must have refused, because in December 1969 he was fined £100 on the drugs charge. His solicitor described him as a man of good character, who did not use drugs, though some of his various acquaintances today remember him as eccentric and even unbalanced. The theme of drugs thus surfaces again in the Chapman story,

44

because Ann certainly did know *a* Peter Johnson from her visits to the Troubadour, the place where she occasionally satisfied her own mild indulgence with cannabis. More significantly, Ann's friend, Nita de Peterson, remembers Johnson – who gave an address in Allingham Street, London, when appearing on the drugs possession charge – as 'a garage owner with a snappy car'.

Michael Hudson, the 'car surgeon' at the Oxford garage, also ran into trouble with drugs. He had worked closely with John Dragoumis, Professor Northedge's protégé. A year after the junta fell, Hudson, together with an Irishman called Jim Brennan, was accused in Greece of drug-running, but charges against Hudson were eventually dropped. It is interesting that negotiations for purchase of the Greek property where they were arrested had been handled by Dragoumis.

The fall-out from the Porsche incident spread quickly. A young Cretan who operated under the code-name 'Takis' was thrown out of Britain. He had been among the early recruits to the Packard network and was present at the meeting in Oxford when the abortive sailing-boat expedition to Greece was discussed. 'Takis' was Nicos Levantakis, now a businessman in Sweden. Faced with the virtual disintegration of his work, Packard began to worry that the substantial store of intelligence accumulated by the police on resistance activity would leak from Britain, via the American connection, to the Greek secret service, with untold consequences not only for his friends but also for members of his family still in Greece. He therefore asked a friend, a sympathetic Labour MP, the late Ray Dobson, to intercede with James Callaghan, the Labour government's Foreign Secretary at the time. The assurances received were evidently sufficient to persuade Packard that he could safely base himself permanently with the resistance movement inside Greece itself, which he almost immediately did. I asked Packard if that was not the equivalent of sitting on a barrel of gunpowder with a lighted match,

45

and he agreed it was certainly 'very delicate'. This can only be an understatement. Packard's early adventures in Cyprus and then in the resistance movement, together with his links to Constantine, made him the subject of considerable curiosity to the CIA as well as British intelligence. Packard had inside knowledge of the clumsy and ill-prepared bid by Constantine to overthrow the junta with the aid of naval officers loyal to the crown at the end of 1968. In London, he had astonished George Yannopoulos by predicting the event with absolute precision. Since the CIA were actually running the show at the KYP headquarters in Athens, it was naive or foolish of Packard to accept, so obviously at face value, the safe-conduct pass transmitted by James Callaghan via Ray Dobson. A more plausible explanation is this: news of Packard's arrival in Greece reached the ears of the KYP, who were then instructed to leave him alone, on the 'devil we know' basis, in order to direct effortless concentration on what was left of the resistance movement inside the country.

Packard remains embittered over the events of the period, believing, as he later told me, that doubts about his loyalty 'contaminated my life'. His powerful attachment to the cause of liberating Greece from the Colonels was expressed in this telling sentence: 'I hold very strongly that nations, and people, should be allowed to work out their own solutions and their own lives and that power or self-interest should not convey rights of interference.' Packard's crusade was against great powers he believed were conspiring to crush freedom and integrity in two small countries – Greece and Cyprus. This extraordinary passion consumed his naval career: his story, in terms of the conflict between the demands upon a serving officer and the pressures which lured him to a rival destiny in a foreign country, has few examples in recent times. There is no convenient slot into which a man like Packard will fit. This will certainly account for any official lapse of memory over the precise circumstances of his departure from the Royal Navy.

Vassili Filias, who remained in prison until his release under general amnesty in 1973, concedes that by 1971 acute disappointment plagued the opposition movement, and resistance inside the country was almost at a standstill. Outside Greece, the divisions sown by Andreas Papandreou had virtually split the opposition.

Reports of torture in junta prisons and secret police cells, fully authenticated by evidence smuggled out of the country, caused surprisingly little distress on the international scene. The world seemed content to look the other way and let the Greeks get on with it. From 1970 onwards, a new factor encouraged American comfort for the regime: the closure of US Air Force bases in Libya and the emergence of strong anti-American sentiments in Turkey bestowed upon Greece a new strategic significance. The US Navy had actually been forced to withdraw from their principal Turkish base at Izmir. The new man in the White House, Richard Nixon, wanted to move urgently to fill the vacuum. In the Vice-President, Spiro Agnew, who had Greek blood in his veins, he had the perfect emissary to acquire a secure base for American ships in a Greek port. Agnew was reinforced by the appointment of Henry Tasca as ambassador in January 1970. Tasca knew from the start that his two priorities in Athens were to secure a safe home port for US naval forces and proceed thereafter to a chart solution in Cyprus. The new British government, Conservative and headed by Edward Heath, offered no objections, grateful for any American initiative which spared it the necessity of any further tiresome mediation between Turks and Greeks.

The Colonels demonstrated the strength of their grip on the country by staging a spectacular show trial of thirty-four members of Democratic Defence, including prominent figures like George A. Manghakis, a future PASOK Justice Minister who became closely involved in the Chapman affair. Many of the accused revoked their confessions in court, claiming that they had been tortured. But cracks were already appearing in the image of an all-powerful junta. August 1970 saw the eruption of an internal crisis, carefully hidden from the world (but not from the CIA) when Papadopoulos received his first serious challenge. The trouble owed its origins to a petty squabble over the senior dictator's matrimonial arrangements and then spread quickly to accusations of complicity in a plot to take the life of Makarios. Papadopoulos surmounted his critics, after a theatrical resignation threat, but his influence had been fatally weakened. Ioannides, brooding behind the apparatus which controlled his private gestapo, resolved that at the next stumble Papadopoulos would fall. Something similar had also been concluded by the CIA who were becoming acutely nervous about Papadopoulos' ability to discharge his secret obligations. The waves which would sweep away the junta were already gathering. The dictators entered 1971 and their fourth year of power in volatile mood.

4 · Curiosity and the Cat

Thou art slave to Fate, chance, kings, and desperate men

— John Donne

The weeks before Ann went to Greece were busy ones, packed with appointments for interviews to win airtime on Radio London. But after barely half a year as a scurrying freelance, she could already see the limits to this parochial round of diary stories. Ann was determined to win more for herself. She was constantly telephoning news editors on the 'Today' programme, flagship of the BBC's national radio network, offering items she had scooped up with her tape-recorder. This eagerness for stories frequently kept her up late at night, usually at the Troubadour, swopping gossip and ideas. A good listener, she retained everything she heard in her neat and well-ordered mind. The evening diet of gossip was sometimes flavoured with politics, and more especially Greek politics after Ann had been introduced to a potentially attractive contact who expressed strong views against the junta. He is remembered as young, smartly-dressed, often too smartly dressed for the Troubadour, and aged about thirty-four. He spoke English well. Some of Ann's acquaintances resented the way that he always brought conversation around to the Colonels and what was happening in Greece. John Parkes, a young teacher who spent most of his evenings on the coffee-bar circuit in Earl's Court, had met Ann in the Troubadour.

'Frankly, I did not like the man at all, and he knew it,' Parkes later told Geoffrey Levy, a *Daily Express* reporter who launched a major investigation into Ann's death. 'Somehow he didn't ring true.' But to Ann he was different and interesting and, much more significantly, he had a story. The young Greek began to tell her about the resistance movement which was working against the Colonels inside and outside the country. In a methodical way she began to clip from the newspapers everything written about Greece. Newspaper cuttings were found in the Cathcart Road flat after her death. Some were nearly four years old, evidently background material contributed by someone else as reports on the political situation were annotated in a red biro but not in Ann's rather untidy style. One clipping, dating back to 1968, the year after the Colonels seized power, referred to Basil Mantzos, an extremely able and successful Greek businessman who had created a major tour firm operating package deals to Greece, and to one of his directors, the Duke of St Albans. This was a small but significant piece in the Chapman jigsaw, because it was Olympic Holidays which would, within a few months, send Ann to Greece as one of its guests.

In late August or early September 1971, John Parkes bumped into Ann one lunchtime in the Old Brompton Road, not far from the Troubadour. She said she was in a hurry and having lunch with someone and, after this short conversation, stepped into an official-looking black saloon car which was waiting at the kerb. The driver, a middle-aged man with greying hair and a military moustache – Parkes thought at the time he was the chauffeur – leaned back to open the rear door. Parkes saw the middle-aged man again, not with Ann but with the persistent young Greek with whom she had made friends at the Troubadour. The two were talking together on the pavement in South Kensington. A few days after that, he again saw Ann with the elder Greek, this time at the Stax hamburger restaurant in the King's Road, Chelsea. They were seated at a table, close to the door.

Five years after Ann's death, Geoffrey Levy's *Daily Express* report named the portly Greek with the military moustache as Christos Lambropoulos, a diplomat attached to the Greek mission in Holland Park. The identification was made by John Parkes who sat in a car while Levy called at a house in Wandsworth. Levy asked Lambropoulos why he had not admitted his meetings with Ann when the Greek and British police were investigating her murder. He denied ever having known the girl and slammed the door in Levy's face, emerging a few minutes later to drive furiously across London to the Holland Park embassy. Levy followed with Parkes, who remained absolutely confident about the accuracy of his sighting, and had also identified a five-year-old photograph of the diplomat. Not surprisingly, because of his job at the embassy, Lambropoulos was well-known to the Greek community in London. He still moves in those circles, and Basil Mantzos, among others, knows him well. In 1963, Lambropoulos had been awarded the MVO, a personal gift of the Queen, for his role in arranging the state visit to London of the Greek King and Queen. George Koutsoumbas, one of the contacts given to Martin Packard by Vassili Filias, was a reservation agent at Olympic Airways in London. Like many employees of the airline, he worked for the resistance as a messenger and his job gave him perfect cover. He told me in Athens that Lambropoulos used to be called 'the surgeon of the Greek embassy – he was involved everywhere and with everything'.

Ann knew perfectly well how to research the background to a story and therefore a contact at the Greek embassy was a logical step. But her driving ambition to uncover what was happening in the resistance movement and connect that to the situation in Greece was already outstripping the range of her experience as a journalist. For that reason she failed to appreciate that everyone working at the Greek embassy dur-

ing the junta years used their eyes and ears to report back to
Athens any snippet of information which could be useful to
the intelligence services. And journalists are always acutely
sensitive subjects for regimes like the military junta then
ruling Greece. So Ann's curiosity and, later, the plans for her
visit, were standard material for the diplomatic bag passing
to and from Athens. For Lambropoulos, 'the surgeon of the
Greek embassy', they were part of the normal diplomatic
trade in intelligence. Now in his seventies and retired from
the embassy since 1979, Lambropoulos continues firmly to
deflect any inquiry about Ann Chapman; he flatly maintains
that he never knew her. So does the Greek embassy, where
officials become markedly animated at the mention of his
name in connection with Ann. When I inquired what duties
Mr Lambropoulos performed as an attaché, I was told bluntly
that such information was the business of the embassy and
no one else. However, while returning to London from a visit
to Athens with Edward and Dorothy Chapman in October
1983, a young Olympic Airways stewardess, who recognized
the Chapmans from their frequent appearances in the Greek
press, asked to speak to me privately at the back of the
aeroplane. She told me that she and her husband, who worked
in the Greek consular service, had rented rooms from Lambropoulos in his house at Wandsworth. On one occasion during
their stay there, the subject of Ann Chapman came up. Lambropoulos confessed it was he who had told the authorities
in Greece about the plans for her visit and when she would
arrive. A crucial addition to that information is Parkes' report
of a meeting between the man he had identified as Lambropoulos and the mysterious young anti-junta Greek who had
befriended Ann in the Troubadour. Parkes would not tell the
reporter Geoffrey Levy who the young Greek was – Levy
thought he seemed afraid. It is now difficult to ask Parkes
any more questions. Like so many of the people who became
involved in the Chapman affair, he has now vanished, it is

thought to America with his wife. Every effort to trace him has failed.

There were persistent reports after Ann's death that she had been meeting Aristotellis ('Tellis') Kotsias, senior Olympic Holidays representative on the Greek trip, before she left London. George Forrest, the resistance sympathiser at Oxford who maintained the Packard link with Peter Johnson's garage, insists Kotsias was involved in the movement. This is not surprising: both Olympic Airways and Olympic Holidays, large employers of Greeks in London, were ideal cover for clandestine operations against the junta. Koutsoumbas, the message carrier at Olympic Airways, talked to Kotsias about Ann late in 1971. Kotsias told him not to ask any more about it 'because it is a very dirty business'.

The links in a chain of events which led to Ann's death were forged early in September. Ann needed to find a way of getting to Greece and had understood enough about the way in which the resistance ran its activities to realize that a trip connected with her work at Radio London would provide the ideal camouflage. Once again, the unofficial information exchange at the Troubadour provided the opening. Someone there – almost certainly the young Greek she had been meeting – knew a PR man called Anthony Dignum, who ran his own small company in John Adam Street. When Ann went there at 12.30 on 9 September she had certainly gone to the right place, because among Dignum's clients was Olympic Holidays. Dignum told a Metropolitan Police inspector in 1977, when inquiries were reopened in London after persistent pressure from Edward Chapman, that it was common practice for companies like Olympic to offer journalists a 'freebie' so that they would write about the trip and generate useful publicity. And it was especially useful at that time because the Greek tourist business had run into a flat patch through a combination of the deepening economic crisis in Britain and the parade-ground economic theories practised by the Colonels. In these circumstances, any news had to be good news. At John Adam Street, Ann was met by another partner, Douglas Smith, and later Dignum joined the two of them for a drink at a pub around the corner. He insists that this was the only time he met Ann. Not long after this meeting, Ann was in the Queensway offices of Olympic Holidays talking to the man who had created the whole enterprise, Basil Mantzos. He told me that the encounter took place 'a few days before her death'. Douglas Smith had popped into the office and asked him to give Ann an interview about tourism and the Greek islands. That completed, Ann left, but Smith apparently looked back into Mantzos' office to say that she would like to go on a trip to Greece. He suggested including her with a group of travel agents who would be leaving about the middle of October to inspect the resorts and hotels selected by Olympic for their 1972 holiday season. Mantzos agreed and told Douglas Smith to make all the arrangements.

The problem with this sequence of events is that it does not fit the record in Ann's diary and nor does it match up with what Ann told her parents, friends and colleagues at Radio London. Dorothy Chapman remembers perfectly well that her daughter had talked on 8 September – the day *before* she went to Anthony Dignum's offices – about going to Greece 'on a big story'. If she had gone to John Adam Street merely to investigate the possibilities of a free trip, as Dignum and Smith both suggested, it is strange that in her own mind she was already convinced that the arrangements had been finalized. Ann was far too precise in her private and professional life to make mistakes like that. Mantzos is quite right that he saw Ann in his office, on 4 October, 'a few days before her death'. But his memory also fails because, as Ann's diary proves, he had two meetings with her, not one. The first was on 21 September, shortly after lunch. There were arrangements for another meeting, or perhaps the date was changed, because a scheduled meeting on 28 September is crossed out. It is clear that when Ann went for the second time to the offices of Basil Mantzos, all the arrangements for the Greek trip had been made. By then, she had already told many people at Radio London that she was setting off later in October and dropped hints to one or two that, although the official purpose was to do something in connection with tourism, she was also going to look into another, much bigger, story. Ann noted in her diary that she was going to 'interview' Mantzos on 4 October, which apparently she did, because at least one witness later heard that recording. But the story of the interview, the way in which it was recorded, and what subsequently happened to it, is another mysterious ingredient in Ann's story.

Dignum, Smith and Mantzos now say that they all thought the interview would be broadcast on Radio London. Ann took with her to Olympic Holidays a small handbag-sized Japanese cassette-recorder, borrowed because her own, similar machine had gone for repair. However, cassette-recorders of that time could not record material to the exacting standards required by broadcasting, and whatever corners were cut at Radio London they did not include transmitting fuzzy interviews. Like all her colleagues at the station, Ann worked professionally with a German-manufactured Uher reel-to-reel recorder, a bulky but highly satisfactory machine much favoured by radio people because of its reliability. Ann's first task on joining the freelance crew at Radio London was to spend a whole day, 7 February, learning how to use the Uher. Ten detailed pages from the instruction manual were later found by her parents. Ann was far too cautious to upset notoriously tetchy news editors with scratchy, low-quality interviews, except in dire emergency of news demands. So why did she use a cassette-recorder if the interview was to be broadcast? The other problem with cassette tapes is that they are difficult to edit unless the recording is first transferred to another machine, an awkward process that Ann was unlikely to want to bother with. All reporters on radio stations do their own editing, a simple enough razor-blade and chalk job when performed on reel-to-reel tape. It is also highly questionable whether such an obvious free plug for Olympic Holidays, minus any 'news peg', would be considered worthy of air-time.

So what were Ann's motives in recording this apparently useless chat with Basil Mantzos? There was a later suggestion that it was commissioned by Olympic Holidays as a promotions exercise, to be recycled throughout the trade bringing good news about Greek tourism. That would certainly account for Ann failing to take her top quality Uher machine to Queensway, and also why she took the small cassetterecorder to Greece. This machine was sent back to London after her death, along with several tapes containing interviews she had made about tourism in Corfu and Athens. But, oddly, the talk with Basil Mantzos in his London office has vanished completely. One travel agent remembered hearing it when Ann played the tape back on a bus in Athens. Edward Chapman sent the tapes for expert examination to a laboratory in London. There it was confirmed that she had recorded over the first interview on the first tape, but the state of the art is such that no one can be absolutely sure what was originally there.

Something else has vanished as well: the professional Uher machine that Ann also took with her to Greece when she left from Gatwick by plane on the morning of Monday 11 October. There is no doubt about this because colleagues at Radio London – including Mike Brook and Charles Murray – recall that she was issued with a Uher although she was not on an official trip and the recorder was actually required by another reporter. Johnnie Longden took her signature for the machine and David Carter, the man who thought 'she had stars in her eyes', saw her with the Uher in Radio London's reception area and chatted with her about the Greek trip. This expensive item of equipment, and about hundred feet of tape, was never returned to London. Both had disappeared from her hotel room and were nowhere to be found in her personal effects. Only the cassette-recorder was returned. Ann had clearly taken the Uher to Greece to record her 'big story'. Her subsequent behaviour – breaking off from the main party for long periods and giving them the impression that she had other interests apart from tourism – confirms her real intentions. Whatever it was that she managed to record on the Uher tapes remains perhaps the most important missing fragment in piecing together the story. There is evidence that Ann's hotel room in Vouliagmeni was thoroughly searched between the point when she left it for the last time and when her body was found. It was almost certainly during this period that the Uher tape-recorder was found and taken into other hands.

Danny Lessing remembers Ann being in a state of unusual excitement before leaving for Greece, and also mentioning that someone was arranging interviews for her. In that context, the diary of the last days of her life raises a vital question. Who was the mysterious 'Chris' that she began meeting in early August and continued to see until shortly before she left for Greece? Ann's parents recall no one of that name, nor do other close friends like Danny Lessing, Gareth Davis and Nita de Peterson. Yet evidently 'Chris' was sufficiently important to meet for dinner and even note the occasions when phone calls were received – just as she did with Gareth Davis. In Ann's diary, appointments for Radio London interviews were always detailed, despite the ragged handwriting, but Chris warrants only the name and a time to meet, though never the place. It is surely significant that 'Chris' appears in her diary about the same time that Ann had been identified meeting the smartly-dressed young Greek together with Christos Lambropoulos, the man from the Greek embassy. She had an evening appointment

with Chris on the day she went to the offices of Anthony Dignum's PR company – only twenty-four hours after telling her
mother about the trip to Greece. Nita de Peterson recalls two
people at the Troubadour called Chris, both English, but she
thought that neither was taking Ann out or likely to meet her
for dinner on private occasions. One possible explanation is the
name 'Chris Tucker', with a telephone number in her address
book. Under pressure from Edward Chapman, Scotland Yard
made random checks on names listed in both her diary and
address book and could apparently trace no one who could
throw light on Ann's contacts in the vital period before she left
London. No one called Chris has ever come forward to help the
Chapmans during their long search for the truth, despite vast
amounts of publicity. There can be no doubt that, whoever he
was, Chris knew why she was making her trip and what she
hoped to get out of it.

Despite the pounding which Packard's organization had received following Special Branch's interception of the Porsche
at Dover, the resistance movement struggled on and London
remained a significant base. The smuggling continued by the
overland route, even though the Oxford base had closed
down. George Yannopoulos thought that the people doing the
smuggling were involved in a 'dangerous and futile activity'.
Some of the emphasis and organizational effort shifted to
Germany, where one of the principal operators was Andreas
Christodulides. Vassili Filias told me that this man worked
out of Germany and France and that he was also a close
confidant of John Dragoumis, who had always been well
integrated into the Packard group.

Christodulides was another peculiar character in the
resistance movement, a backer of Andreas Papandreou who
was later rewarded for his loyalty with a place on the PASOK
executive committee, plus the directorship of the government-
controlled press agency. Years later, all this went awry when,

in one of the few such scandals ever to rock Greek society, Christodulides was accused of being a transvestite who spent his evenings in low-life Athens night-clubs. Christodulides furiously denied the accusation, cleared his name and returned to his job at the press agency. Photographs which appeared in Greek newspapers were certainly not clear enough to identify him positively and political circles in Greece today suggest that the whole affair blew up when he became a victim of one of the periodic eruptions inside PASOK caused by rival figures jostling for power.

The German connection is, however, important in one other respect. Shortly after Ann's death, a German social democrat code-named Karl – who specialized in spiriting people from the Colonels' clutches – surfaced with the claim that Ann had been instructed by Greek intelligence in London to make contact with a certain Greek once she arrived in the country. He would then hand her information to bring back to London. This was either a disinformation exercise – of which there were many – or proof that the resistance was riddled with people betraying the opposition to the junta, the CIA or British intelligence, or a combination of all three. Ann had indeed arranged to meet people in Greece who had nothing to do with tourism and she had also been spotted in London talking to people who were on different sides of the fence. No resistance movement is watertight – as Roger Williams discovered when the police swooped at Dover – but Ann had made the fatal mistake of appearing to both sides as the object of suspicion. That is why she was already caught in a trap before she even boarded the Corfu-bound plane at Gatwick. Orders had already gone out to the KYP to tail her from the moment she arrived. And the hackles of the resistance movement had risen sharply out of the fear that she was a British agent or spy on a dangerous mission of penetration.

Ann Chapman was therefore doomed from the moment she set foot in the country.

5 · A Passage to Greece

Like one, that on a lonesome road
Doth walk in fear and dread

—Samuel Taylor Coleridge, *The Ancient Mariner*

Ann's preparations for the journey to Greece warrant a special note in her diary for Friday 8 October, just three days before she was due to leave. Her weekend shopping list included a mains adapter and batteries for the small borrowed Sony cassette-recorder and some Greek currency. Under the heading of 'news info', she prompted herself with a note about 'Greece – tourism, culture, arts, traditions', and also, 'Women in prison'. There is another entry which acquired a particular significance for the few days she spent in Corfu, the first stop of the trip: 'Find name of Fiat garage.' Ann hired a car at a Fiat garage on the island for a journey which has never been properly explained.

The weather in Greece can be unpredictable in October, sometimes warm and sunny but often cool and wet. Ann took no risks and prepared for any climate. Property found in her hotel room included autumn suits and dresses, slacks, light blouses and scarves, together with sun-tan lotion and swimming costumes. She took two paperbacks, *A Passage to India* and *Cancer Ward*.

On the weekend of 9 and 10 October, the other members of the party were also happily anticipating their expedition to Greece, promoted by Olympic Holidays as 'Agents educational tour number two'. Fourteen representatives of mostly small travel agencies scattered around Britain had been signed up for an intensive ten-day schedule which would take in Corfu, Athens and Crete. It appeared to be a perfectly normal promotional exercise, of the kind that all of them had experienced before and would regard as one of the attractive perks of working in High Street travel agencies that supply most of the business for firms like Olympic Holidays. The programme was sent out by Olympic in advance: a 3 a.m. flight to Corfu on Monday 11 October from London's customary package-tour airport, Gatwick. There would be three nights in Corfu, with the days spent looking at hotels and beaches. They would leave for Athens on 14 October, and a similar pattern would be repeated before leaving the following Sunday for Crete. The return to London was scheduled for Tuesday 19 October, although Ann's diary has a question mark over that date and she evidently considered staying on in Greece for a few more days. She lists flights from Crete to Rhodes on 22 October, and on 27 October from Rhodes to Athens, and on to London. Ann had mentioned to a few people that she might extend her visit and some thought she had talked about a ski-ing holiday afterwards – which is unlikely, because October is far too early to look for useful snow in Europe. Of much greater importance are Ann's remarks to her mother when she called at the Putney home on the evening of Sunday 10 October. They already knew she was looking for some kind of special news story but now she was much more precise. Dorothy Chapman recalls: 'As she was going up the stairs to the bathroom, she told me, "I have just been given a big story – they tell me it will make my name in journalism all over the world."' She seemed excited. The Chapmans were puzzled over what Ann had said, and for a moment she seemed prepared to say more. But then she cut herself off: 'I'll tell you all about it when I get back.' Except over the business of moving into a flat with Danny Lessing, Dorothy Chapman had not been used to reticence from her daughter. Ann's parents have bitterly regretted that they did not press her to explain more; but just before leaving the house, she did convey to them a hint of her own evidently increasing fears. She paused, and said she was wondering whether she should go to Greece after all. This was the last occasion on which the Chapmans saw their daughter.

The Olympic party left Gatwick at three o'clock on the morning of the 11th, arriving in Corfu just after dawn. Tellis Kotsias met the party at the airport and they all travelled to the hotel by bus. There was time only for a brief wash and brush-up and breakfast before the travel agents were whisked away to begin their inspection tour of local hotels and beaches. Ann stayed behind and went off to locate the Fiat garage and arrange the car hire. From the moment she had been identified at passport control in Corfu airport, agents had been deployed to watch her every move, following the tip-off to the intelligence service from the Greek embassy in London. In the evening, the hotel management offered drinks and dinner, rounded off with Greek folk dancing and music in the lounge. Everyone seems to have gone off to bed in a jolly mood. Ann found herself sharing a room with a young Olympic courier, Lynda Nichol; an arrangement which upset one or both of them because, by the time the group reached the Pine Hill Hotel in Kavouri, both were insisting on their own rooms. Lynda Nichol has puzzled every investigator into the story, including Edward Chapman. Not long after Ann's death, Lynda Nichol left Olympic Holidays. Edward Chapman ran her to ground, after a long search, living on the island of Crete and working with a local travel company. The encounter between the two – recorded by a Greek news magazine whose entourage included a photographer complete with tele-photo lens – was brief and unrevealing. Nichol was defensive and reluctant to talk about Ann. She insisted that she had forgotten most of what had happened at the Pine Hill Hotel. Whatever the cause of the dispute between the two girls, the dispute itself was later useful to the Greek authorities: the story that drugs were found among Ann's possessions at Kavouri conveniently matched the image of a flighty young foreigner willing to indulge in casual sex, and the fact that she had quarrelled with her room mate seemed only to confirm this.

Tellis Kotsias could have been a vital witness; he might have explained why the two girls fell out, and why he agreed to separate them. But he too is dead, having drowned in the river Thames in circumstances never fully explained.

Shirley Butler, the other Olympic courier in the party, is keeping whatever she does know to herself. Remembered as a 'natural, happy girl', she has vanished, making contact with Edward Chapman only once in fifteen years, following a public appeal I made at the beginning of the European Parliament's inquiry into Ann's death. In a brief telephone conversation she spoke anxiously of wanting to meet Edward Chapman and talk to him about Ann. Then she hung up, without leaving a number. Chapman has never heard from her again.

John Talbot, a travel agent from Bournemouth, thought that Kotsias and Lynda Nichol had been deputed to arrange appointments for Ann with 'interesting locals'. If she was dependent upon Lynda Nichol for help, why – in a notable departure from her usual agreeable character and composure – did Ann fall out with a vital source of important contacts and information? John Talbot was the only one of the party to offer Edward Chapman positive help from the moment he returned from Greece. He had seen that from the start Ann had been her 'own master', setting off with a tape-recorder to work on a brief which he assumed was connected with her job at Radio London.

At least one of Ann's missions on Corfu can be confirmed. This was an interview with an 'influential lady', an authority on the history of the island, at the Achilleon Palace Hotel. It survives among the Sony tapes which found their way back to England – but, oddly enough, it is exactly in the place where the talk with Basil Mantzos should be. The interview appears to have been harvested during Ann's eighty-kilometre drive around the island in the Fiat car on Tuesday the 12th. Where else she went remains unresolved, although without doubt Kotsias knew.

Wherever Ann did go that day, and whoever she met, she was worried and distracted for the remainder of the stay in Corfu. An extraordinarily precise testament of Ann's feelings during that period was recorded by a young Greek barman working at Olympic Holidays' base, the Cavalieri Hotel. His evidence, given to the island police when inquiries were initiated shortly after her death, was not repeated at the trial of Nicholas Moundis, or at any of the subsequent re-trials. Yet it remains a chilling record of Ann's disturbed state of mind as she commenced inquiries into her 'big story'. On the evening of the 12th, a Tuesday, a dinner had been arranged by Kotsias at a local taverna, the Xenychti. The idea was to give the travel agents a taste of the local night-life – simple, noisy, cheap and very Greek. Kotsias went ahead of the party, hitching a lift on a motor scooter with the young hotel barman, George Balatsinos. Ann arrived with the rest of the party about an hour later and everyone settled down to a typical Greek taverna evening. All, that is, except Ann. Balatsinos was attracted to the 'young brunette, slim and Ann by name' as soon as she walked through the door – a not especially remarkable display of curiosity from a young man working in a job where foreign girls might offer interesting opportunities. But Ann was not interested in him or anyone else. In his statement to local gendarmerie detectives, Balatsinos said: 'Ann was showing that something was occupying her mind and notwithstanding the fact that the group were amusing themselves and she herself took part in the amusements, nevertheless she was downcast and she showed no interest in the surroundings or the people.' Others might have been discouraged but Balatsinos spoke good enough English to get her to dance, 'even though her attitude was totally at variance with the environment and the jolly atmosphere'. He tried to get her to say what was wrong, and she replied abruptly 'nothing'. Others in the party also tried to cheer her up and fared no better. The party finally broke up at about four o'clock in the morning but Balatsinos left at around 2.30, together with a friend, Ioannis Rigenas, who had also been talking and dancing with Ann. Both were struck by the peculiar behaviour of the young English girl and they talked about the 'depressed state she was in' all the way back to the hotel.

There were more peculiarities in Ann's behaviour the following day. Balatsinos' job behind the bar at the Cavalieri gave him a useful view of the lounge and all who went in or out. Coming on duty shortly after five o'clock on the Wednesday evening, he was surprised to see Ann sitting by herself in the lounge for about an hour, with her head in a book. He saw that she wore the 'same sad look' she had displayed in the taverna: 'She was staring with a glassy look, straight in front of her and then, with a jerk, returning to her book.' Balatsinos went on serving drinks to early-evening customers, watching Ann until she went up to her room. Later that night there were more festivities at the taverna. Again, Ann went along with the rest of the company. She was obviously reluctant to stay alone at the hotel. She was also clearly not enjoying herself, remaining withdrawn and depressed, and keeping out of the fun.

Balatsinos observed that a young Englishman – well-spoken, fair, medium build – was taking a special interest in Ann. 'He followed Ann with his eyes,' Balatsinos told the local detectives. This young Englishman was staying at the same hotel, the Cavalieri, because, when the party broke up, he shared a seat with Ann on the return bus journey. This description fits Nick Clarkson, a young travel agent from Exchange Travel in Manchester. Balatsinos remarked, 'He was not a likeable man.'

If any serious attempt had ever been undertaken by the authorities in Greece to track down Ann's killers, her behaviour in Corfu left important clues. The row with Lynda Nichol, which led to the pair of them splitting off into separate rooms, looks suspiciously like an attempt to isolate Ann. Was some kind of dispute therefore artificially engineered? Lynda Nichol made only a brief statement to police officers after Ann's body was found and never received a summons to the subsequent trial of Moundis. Six years later, she told the Metropolitan Police in London that, since Ann's murder, she had suffered 'a great deal of harassment both at business and at home' and for that reason she was reluctant even to disclose her private address or telephone number. She remained insistent that she never met Ann before the trip to Greece, but clearly she was in a position to provide important clues about those few days in Corfu, and to shed light on subsequent claims concerning drugs allegedly found in Ann's room. The testimony of the barman, Balatsinos, concerning Ann's depressed mood was also suppressed. One possible reason for this lies in the confusing method by which the investigation was actually pursued.

Until 1984, the Greek police were divided into two entirely separate forces: a national gendarmerie concentrated mostly in the rural areas and the islands, and the Athens central command. There was always powerful rivalry between the two. Initial inquiries into Ann's death were mounted, appropriately, by the gendarmerie but, after a short period, the case was transferred to the Athens police. There is clear evidence that much of the important material collected in the early stages of the inquiry by gendarmerie officers – like the interview in Corfu with Balatsinos – either never found its way to the Athens police headquarters or, having reached there, was promptly discarded. In any case most of it would never conceivably match up with the attempt to implicate Moundis. After he had turned private detective, Edward Chapman was the first to focus on the significance of the invoice for the care hire on Corfu, which he located among his daughter's belongings. No one pursued that vital line of inquiry, linked as it is to the entry in Ann's diary which indicated that she had to find the name of a particular Fiat garage before she even set out on the journey.

Apologists have tried to suggest that sloppy police work was entirely to blame for a trail of clues which were lost, ignored or simply thrown away. Certainly there was a good deal of that; but deliberate attempts at disinformation and concealment of important evidence played a far more significant role. One example of this was the bizarre red herring dragged into the story years later when Edward Chapman received a packet of papers – purporting to be secret US intelligence documents on Turkey – accompanied by a letter with an indecipherable signature which said: 'Your daughter would have brought these documents back to London if she had lived ... I know who is the real killer.' The State Department in Washington confirmed that the papers, dealing with the activities of various anti-government forces in Turkey, were indeed genuine; but at the time of Ann's death they were already eight years old and fit only for the historical archives. There was nothing in them to create the slightest ripple of a story for a young journalist trying to make her name, still less attempting to penetrate the intelligence networks in Greece or anywhere else. The episode was another exercise designed to throw Edward Chapman off the track of his daughter's killers.

The Corfu chapter is vital in unravelling the story of what

eventually happened to Ann because it proves that, even before she arrived in Athens, she had become fully aware of the risks she was taking – either because a contact already made on the island had unsettled her, or she had noticed she was being followed everywhere.

Ann commenced the next stage of the journey, to Athens, by driving the hired car to Corfu airport early on the morning of Thursday 14 October. With the rest of the party, she boarded the 8.20 scheduled flight for the short hop to the Greek capital. Kotsias had a bus waiting and, after briefly looking in at two other hotels selected by Olympic for the coming year's programme, he checked the party into the Pine Hill Hotel at Kavouri. They had the rest of the day to themselves, but other eyes were already watching Ann. She had arrived in a capital swarming with police activity as the Colonels prepared to receive their important visitor from America, Vice-President Spiro Agnew. Extra troops and police had been drafted into the capital area from all over Greece and the city itself was effectively shut off inside a cordon sanitaire, with other special forces deployed around the airport and the Vouliagmeni area, where Ann was staying. It was the largest police operation since the Colonels' seizure of power. The presence inside the security zone of what the junta believed to be a BBC reporter travelling incognito was already well-known to the intelligence authorities.

The visit of Agnew had placed extra pressure on the man-power of KYP and its military equivalent, ESA, and in order to see what Ann was up to, gendarmerie officers were brought in to fill the gaps. One of these was a low-ranking officer called Felouris, based at Raffina, who told me in 1984 that he had been instructed by his seniors to follow Ann's movements on Saturday, 16 October, when the Olympic group was due to take a short sea trip to the island of Hydra. He was shown a photograph and told not to speak to Ann, only to report back whom she spoke to. In another episode of curiously misplaced witnesses and evidence, the testimony of Felouris was never heard at the trial, and the deposition he made has been lost. The travel agent, John Talbot, writing to Mr Chapman shortly after Ann's death, also made a note of 'unusual' people around the hotel. Shortly after lunch on the 14th – when the party had its afternoon off – he and three others strolled down to the rather scruffy, run-down beach at Kavouri. They found Ann already there, sun-bathing. Talbot's attention was distracted by a muscular figure indulging in physical exercise – a fitness fanatic, he thought, and almost certainly Greek. After about an hour, towards three o'clock, as the afternoon began to turn chilly, Ann set off back along a steep path which led directly to the hotel. Talbot and the others do not remember seeing Ann again that day: but he thought the figure who was exercising only a few yards away from Ann represented one of those incidents which might have had considerable significance 'if only we had all been interviewed prior to leaving Greece or on arrival in the UK'. It remains astonishing that, with a murder on their hands, the gendarmerie made only cursory inquiries among the Olympic party before letting them all fly straight back to London. Even more disturbing is the fact that, of the entire party, Kotsias alone was summoned back to give evidence at the trial of Moundis.

Friday 15 October, the last day of Ann's life, saw the travel agents boarding a bus for the half-hour ride into Athens to visit seven of the top-ranking hotels in the city centre. Ann went with them but broke off from the party almost immediately. She declared that one of her jobs that day was to interview the president of the Greek tourist organization. No one was unduly concerned that Ann was off on her own again. She had already been nicknamed 'Radio London'. But she rejoined the group at odd points and two of these assume particular significance in piecing together the last hours of her life. The travel agents lunched at the Hotel Stanley and then at about three they set off on a short coach excursion to the Acropolis. According to the recollection of John Talbot, Ann met up with them at the Parthenon and rode back into central Athens on the group bus. A few of the party inquired, in the normal way, what she had been doing and Ann responded by playing back some of the tapes she had recorded. She was sitting towards the centre of the coach and John Talbot was among those who heard quite clearly that one of the recordings was with 'Mr Basil Mantzos of Olympic Holidays, prior to leaving London'. It is this interview which has vanished or been erased by recording over it. The original purpose of the talk seems to have been no more than to establish Ann's credentials as a bona fide journalist but the fact that it, together with several other tapes, has never been found is another vital element in the search and seizure of some of her belongings which occurred after her death.

The next stop for the party was a late afternoon reception at the offices of Aeolian Travel, at that time a local travel agency operation – which Olympic Holidays used – and run jointly by Basil Mantzos and his Athens partner, Dimitri Lalelis. When I talked to him in 1984, Mr Lalelis remembered the occasion well because he recalled being especially busy that afternoon and was not keen for the party of British travel agents to hang around his office too long. It is the Greek custom to offer a few drinks and some snacks to visitors. Accordingly, a few bottles of the traditional drink, ouzo, were put out but Mr Lalelis did not follow his normal practice of phoning to the café downstairs to send up a selection of appetizers. It is significant, with later events in mind, that none of the party saw Ann eat anything.

Kotsias asked Lalelis to help Ann fix some interviews with tourist officials and it may have been the shadowy figure of Brian Rawson who was entrusted with this task. Rawson was a direct employee of Olympic and lived at the time at 34

Diakou Street, not far from the city's noisy Plaka night-club district which straddles a shoulder of the Acropolis hill. He seems to have had a wife and two children living there with him. A month after Ann's death Rawson departed abruptly for Australia, it was declared, but all inquiries there have failed to reveal any British immigrant who arrived with that name, even if he changed it afterwards. The only certainty about Brian Rawson is that he was among the official partici-pants at the reception in Aeolian Travel's offices and that, after telephoning the British embasssy on Sunday morning, the 17th, to announce that Ann was missing, he was never heard of again. It is one of the most remarkable vanishing tricks in the entire Chapman story, because not only has Brian Rawson disappeared, but so have his wife and children. Lalelis recalls Rawson as a 'young and sympathetic' sort of individual who sold tours on commission and who left the country in November of that year. In normal circumstances, it is very hard for cautious guardians like the British govern-ment to mislay citizens, particularly four of them at once. But persistent inquiries at Olympic Holidays drew no result for either Edward Chapman or myself, neither did extensive press appeals over the years for Rawson to come forward and help in the investigation. Edward Chapman wrote to the Home Office in London asking them to send on a letter to his last known address, which was agreed, but no reply was ever received. Twelve years after Ann's death, her father was still looking for the elusive Brian Rawson. His local MP, David Mellor, also made inquiries, but the reply from Home Office minister Lord Belstead was typical of the official attitude: 'Passport regulations require that information obtained as a result of passport applications should remain strictly confi-dential.' To a citizen perhaps, but the European Parliament was also refused details of Rawson's last known address and an attempt to trace him through social security records kept on the national computer at Newcastle proved fruitless. In

1977, when the Metropolitan Police trawled through the affair again, no search was mounted for Rawson. Lord Belstead's determination to protect confidentiality of passport applications was misplaced in the matter of murder.

So who was the mysterious Mr Rawson? From what little is known, he appears to have been an innocent figure working on commission to sell coach tours and trips around the Aegean bays. But why, then, did he assume the responsibility for telephoning the British embassy on the Sunday morning to report Ann's disappearance, after what the very thin record available suggests was only the briefest of acquaintances with her? This is even stranger when judged by the fact that the 'Athens suburbs security sub-directorate' had already put out an all-points call for Ann the previous day, Saturday, as a result of the concern shown by Kotsias when Ann failed to appear on the Saturday morning.

There was one event on that Saturday afternoon, when Ann was already dead, which is revealing about what had happened in the offices of Aeolian Travel the previous day. Shortly after two o'clock on Saturday the 16th, Janet Damen, the BBC's official representative in Athens and a young woman of about Ann's age, received a puzzling telephone call, details of which she later gave to the police. The call was from the offices of Aeolian Travel, from a man speaking English. He asked Janet Damen if she was working with the BBC and, if so, whether she knew Miss Chapman. He added that Ann wished 'to write something about Agnew for the BBC'. Damen registered surprise to the caller because the BBC foreign news desk in London had not commissioned her to file anything in connection with the Agnew visit – which had, in fact, already begun. She also declared her surprise that another BBC reporter was apparently in Athens with a group of travel agents, and evidently very interested in Spiro Agnew. Janet Damen's caller went on to indicate *his* concern that something had perhaps happened to Ann. He sounded anxious when he said that she had not returned to her hotel the previous evening, although all her belongings were still there. Janet Damen told the caller to ring the British embassy and gave him the number. After the Athens newspapers had reported the discovery of Ann's body, she called Aeolian Travel the following Wednesday and talked to Dimitri Lalelis, who agreed it was he who had telephoned on the previous Saturday. This evidence – like so much else, ignored at the Moundis trial – indicates that Ann had begun to talk about her interest in Agnew. She could not have imagined she could simply pop around to the Vice-President's well-protected residence and enjoy a cosy little chat with him. The visit was not secret, although its motives were, but talk and chatter about it from a BBC reporter, complete with tape-recorder, who was travelling about Athens with a group of travel agents, was sufficient to rattle nerves everywhere inside a state equally obsessed with external threat and internal conspiracy.

6 · Journey to Nowhere

> Some circumstantial evidence is very strong, as when you find a
> trout in the milk.
>
> —Henry Thoreau

On the evening of Friday the 15th, Kotsias had arranged an
evening supper party at the Electra Hotel in central Athens.
Most of the party agreed to go directly there and not to bother
with a bus or taxi journey back to the Pine Hill Hotel. But
Nicholas Clarkson and Ann both decided to return to wash
and change. The pair went together by bus. According to
Clarkson's later recollection of the trip, Ann was not especially communicative and they chatted, a little stiffly, about
her adventures in Afghanistan. The driver on the route that
evening, Panaghiotis Georgiou, is an important witness, because he clearly remembered a young English couple – 'the
man about twenty-five with blond hair which had curled, the
young woman aged about twenty-five to thirty-five and brown
faced' – boarding the bus and getting off at the St Nicholas
stop. From there they had a two- or three-minute walk to the
hotel. The stop itself, with a small shelter and bordered by a
low wall, was alongside the patch of scrubby wasteland where
Ann's body was discovered three days later. The bus driver,
Georgiou, was also absolutely precise that on the return
journey into Athens, there was no young woman waiting at
the St Nicholas stop; indeed, he picked no one up there at

all. The reception manager at the Pine Hill Hotel, George Malavetas, recalled the pair returning to the hotel at, he thought, about 7.30. Both went upstairs, Ann to room 51, which she occupied alone, Clarkson to his room next door – the rooms were close enough together for Ann to call out to Clarkson several times from her balcony, asking what time it was. He had the impression that Ann was rushing to catch a bus back into Athens to meet up with the rest of the Olympic party. The staff at the hotel's reception desk also had a similar idea, because Ann reappeared asking how she could quickly get back into Athens. Coming from a young woman who was normally so precise, the query was surprising, because she had only just returned to the hotel by bus, to the local stop, within the last hour. Had she changed her mind within that hour about going to the Electra, or had she never intended to return in the first place? Basil Kasimatis, the hotel manager, told the police that he explained to Ann about bus schedules and the location of the bus stop. According to Kasimatis, Ann rushed off immediately, at around 8.15 – although Clarkson, who had gone downstairs to the bar, put her departure about twenty-five minutes earlier. Kasimatis contributed one further vital piece of evidence concerning Ann's clothes. She left, he said, in a 'Chinese-style' mini-skirt. Yet Nicholas Clarkson insisted that she was wearing trousers with a zig-zag pattern at the bottom. However, quite different trousers, blue jeans, were eventually found at the murder site, and the zig-zag trousers turned up among Ann's belongings when they were returned to London.

Sitting drinking Greek beer at the bar – where he remained for most of the evening – Clarkson saw Ann walk out of the door, one of the last witnesses who actually saw her alive. When Nicholas Moundis was accused of killing Ann months later, the prosecution alleged that she had walked the few metres down the slight hill to the St Nicholas bus stop and, while sitting there on the low wall waiting for the bus to arrive, that she was approached by Moundis. This encounter led to her death after a protracted struggle on the nearby wasteland.

It is clear that Ann had enough time to walk from the hotel to the bus stop to catch the evening bus into Athens, if that was what she actually intended. But, as the evidence of the bus driver reveals, there were no passengers waiting at the stop when he drove by. The prosecution thought that they could nail Moundis because he had certainly been in the area for most of the day, first to keep a date with a girl who did not turn up, and then to prowl about in the local woodland spying on courting couples, his favourite leisure pastime. The bus driver did notice a man crossing the main road near the stop, a man bearing by later accounts a resemblance to Moundis. This individual waved the bus on – he was crossing the road from the direction of the Pine Hill Hotel towards the stop. Even if this figure was Moundis, it does not help the case against him because, as the autopsy on Ann's body proved, she was not killed until several hours later – by which time Moundis was far away and had a reliable alibi to prove it. What remains certain is that when Ann left the hotel lobby she did not hurry down the road to the bus stop but went outside to meet someone who was waiting for her by arrangement – hence the rush when she got back to the hotel and the constant interrogation of her room neighbour, Clarkson, for the exact time. Other important evidence confirms interesting movements outside the hotel at about the time that Ann was leaving. At around twenty minutes to seven, fitting more or less precisely Clarkson's memory of when she left, an Athens taxi driver, Ioannis Phytas, picked up two fares at the taxi rank in nearby Vouliagmeni, about two kilometres from the Pine Hill Hotel at Kavouri. Both were young and apparently male, although there is some confusion in the translator's notes of Phytas' evidence about the sex of one of them. The first of this pair got out of the taxi after about one kilometre but the second asked to be driven on and dropped about fifty metres short of the Pine Hill Hotel. Phytas said: 'At that point we arrived at about ten minutes or five minutes to eight o'clock and I saw, in the road, a woman who was waiting. As soon as my fare saw her, he told me to stop.' The two spoke immediately, the woman asking why he was late. Allowing for the poor light in a dark street, Phytas could see well enough that this woman had longish hair, falling over her shoulders from an oval face, and held in place by a clip. She was well dressed, he thought, in dark trousers – like those discovered later in the field near the bus stop. The description fits Ann very well indeed. The man who met her – clearly the meeting was anticipated – was tall, about twenty-four years old, with a dark complexion. He wore glasses and was dressed in a sports jacket and trousers. His friend, quite obviously the same man who had got out of the taxi a kilometre back down the road, was of similar age, short, plump and round-faced. In a key section of his statement to the police, Phytas said: 'They must be residents in the area, from what I understood.' The significance of this remark became clear when it was later confirmed that the resistance movement had a 'safe house' just a few kilometres down the road, in Vouliagmeni. Taxi drivers often have to be patient with the curious demands of their customers and this short journey contained several odd events. For instance, Phytas remembered very clearly that, shortly after setting off from the taxi rank in Vouliagmeni, one of his passengers spotted two women near the local petrol station evidently trying to signal the taxi to stop. It is the custom to share taxis in Greece and drivers often infuriate their customers by stopping to pack even more fares aboard, so Phytas would have been glad of more custom in this out-of-the-way spot. He stopped. One of the men got out of the taxi and talked to the two women, in English. A small, white, British-manufactured car, a Morris Cooper, then drew up. Inside were two Greeks, one with a moustache and the other with a beard. By great coincidence these people apparently all knew each other, although Phytas could not hear everything that was said. The passengers in the Morris Cooper collected the two women and then set off in the general direction of Athens. Phytas resumed his journey to the Pine Hill Hotel, first dropping one of his passengers.

All this activity in the vicinity of the hotel, just at the time when Ann was last seen alive, was suppressed by the investigating authorities. Phytas' evidence was discredited by the campaign of disinformation which is so familiar throughout this tale. The police alleged he was an unreliable witness and often told lies. This slur does not withstand close examination. Why should Phytas have 'told lies' about events whose significance would not have been clear to him? Equally, he had no motive to fabricate the story. He gave evidence to Major Goundras of the gendarmerie on 21 October, three days after Ann's body had been found near the bus stop. The conviction of Moundis lay months away over the horizon. Had Ann returned safe and well to London, Phytas would have forgotten all about the events around Vouliagmeni that evening. Instead, the court which convicted Moundis preferred to stifle Phytas' evidence because it totally contradicted the case against the man on trial. What Phytas remembered proved that Ann had never set off for the bus stop but instead was picked up by a man who was waiting for her outside the Pine Hill Hotel, and whom she fully expected to meet there.

At the Electra Hotel, where the Olympic party was dining, no one except Kotsias was surprised that Ann had not appeared. John Talbot remembered afterwards: 'I do not believe anyone was unduly concerned because she was a free agent.' In other words, 'Radio London' was probably hard at work with her tape-recorder again. After rounding off the evening in a taverna, the party set off by bus back to the Pine Hill Hotel. Talbot, who was sharing a room with another travel agent, was informed by this colleague that 'we had been reprimanded for making too much noise as someone had banged on the door – he said it was "Radio London"'. However, discussing this point later they agreed it was probably an English couple who 'we believed had the adjoining room to Ann'. Room 51 was – or should have been – empty at that time; yet the noise which disturbed the English holiday-makers had come from this supposedly silent room. In view of the later confusion over Ann's belongings – including the discrepancies in her dress, the disappearance of tapes and the Uher tape-recorder – the event assumes significance. At this stage, no one knew that Ann was missing, let alone actually dead. Yet her room was already being ransacked, noisily, by somebody who had managed to enter without arousing the suspicion of the hotel management downstairs. Alternatively, it might have been possible for a reasonably athletic individual to scale up to the second floor of the hotel and get into Ann's room from the balcony. Talbot was never asked about this incident by the police – although he was quick to tell Edward Chapman. The following morning Kotsias appeared distracted over Ann's failure to show up. She was not necessarily expected to take part in the trip to Hydra – for which the party was awoken at 6.30 – but the night porter was concerned that he could get no reply to a knock on the door of room 51. Malavetas, the reception manager, was informed and tried knocking as well, still getting no response. Kotsias rushed off to the waiting ship by taxi, leaving Malavetas to keep trying. He got the key and entered the room, but found no sign of Ann and the bed clearly unslept in.

By the evening, Ann's disappearance had been reported to the police by Kotsias and Clarkson, who both went to the local police station. The security section for the Athens suburbs police district circulated a message to the aliens centre on Saturday night stating that she had failed to return to the Pine Hill Hotel. A message was then despatched to all ports and airports with an instruction to look out for a young woman answering Ann's description wearing 'a white and red dress with white sleeves and collar' – yet further confusion over her clothing. From Hydra Kotsias kept in touch with the Pine Hill Hotel throughout the day to discover what, if anything, was happening about Ann. Someone also told Dimitri Lalelis at Aeolian Travel, because shortly after lunch he was talking to Janet Damen about Ann's interest in Spiro Agnew and her failure to return to the hotel. No one informed the British embassy at this stage; this task was assumed by Brian Rawson when he telephoned the duty officer at around eleven o'clock the following day, Sunday. Kotsias kept his fears to himself while the party cruised around the local waters of the Aegean – none of the travel agents realizing at this stage that anything serious had occurred. Everyone assumed that Ann had simply gone off on her own again. But Nicholas Clarkson thought Kotsias was distinctly uneasy throughout the day, and in the evening the pair of them went to the local police station in Vouliagmeni. By Sunday morning – when the majority of the party had become aware that Ann was still missing – matters had reached a crucial stage, because the whole group was due to exit shortly to Crete, the last stage of their Greek journey. John Talbot recalls that 'one of the girls' – presumably either Lynda Nichol or Shirley Butler, the other courier from Olympic Holidays – went into room 51 and searched it, finding, it was said, the small Sony tape-recorder, many cigarettes and a 'quantity of drugs in a suitcase'. Discussion became rife and everyone speculated where Ann might be. The talk ranged over the visit of Spiro Agnew to Athens and the possibility that the drugs supposedly found in her suitcase might have led her into awkward company. At home in Putney, Edward Chapman and his wife still knew nothing of the developing crisis. No one seems to have considered putting a call through to them to see if Ann had by some chance gone quietly back to London – which, since she was understood by the party to be a journalist, might not have been too surprising. No one at Radio London was told that one of its reporters was missing. Olympic Holidays in London are insistent they received no message from their senior man on the spot, Kotsias, not even after Brian Rawson had telephoned the British embassy, until news was sent to Mr Basil Mantzos the following Tuesday that Ann's body had actually been found. The embassy, which might have displayed a natural concern over a journalist's disappearance in a country run by a military junta – particularly during a visit by the American Vice-President – also failed to contact the Chapmans, or anyone else. By now Ann had been dead for twenty-four hours.

The Greek embassy in London had received a message on Sunday, not just that Ann had vanished, but that subsequently something extremely unfortunate had happened to her. A day or two later, while still attempting to come to terms with the appalling shock of Ann's death, the Chapmans received an official letter of consolation from the embassy, containing a most revealing passage: 'Ever since Sunday, all of us here have followed the news of this reprehensible crime with great concern and anxiety.' On Sunday, all that was officially known about Ann was the fact of her disappearance. Her body, it would later be maintained, was still lying in the scrubland near the bus stop at St Nicholas, to be discovered on Monday by a couple searching for edible snails. How odd, then, that the Greek embassy, far away in London knew all about a 'reprehensible crime'.

Meanwhile, concern had been mounting steadily among the Olympic party, who all now knew that the police had been informed. But no police arrived at the Pine Hill Hotel to mount an investigation, or to track the route that Ann was supposed to have taken on Friday evening to the local bus stop. There is no record of any police activity whatsoever on Sunday, or indeed until Monday when the body was found, except that John Talbot did note something curious in the hotel lobby in the early hours of Sunday morning. Passing the reception area Talbot saw a uniformed policeman. It was the first – and last – he saw as the affair developed. On Sunday, Kotsias decided that the party should go on to Crete as planned. The two women couriers were delegated to pack up Ann's belongings which then found their way to the offices of Dimitri Lalelis at Aeolian Travel. If the police had intended to search Ann's room properly, looking for fingerprints or any other interesting material, the various forays in and out of that room (quite apart from the unauthorized nocturnal investigation on the Friday evening) had completely destroyed whatever useful evidence there might have been. The Olympic party, in sober mood and talking anxiously about Ann, boarded the bus and then jetted off to Crete on the 9.20 flight.

On Monday unsettled weather worsened and turned to rain. In Crete, Kotsias and the others heard no news of Ann from Athens. At Kavouri, the highway running past the St Nicholas bus stop was busy with the usual Monday traffic. The scrubland where Ann's body was found contains only a few short and stubbly trees, with no high walls to conceal its generally uninteresting features. Yet, if we are to believe the official report, the body of a fairly well-built young woman, still wearing some of her colourful clothes, was lying in an exposed position just a few metres from the bus stop. Anyone walking down the slight hill from the Pine Hill Hotel towards the stop has an uninterrupted view of the spot, which remains virtually unchanged today. At the rear of the site lies a mud-track road, used for access to the few isolated houses which existed in the area then. This track did, and still does, command an even better view of anything that might be in the field. It is an astonishing, unbelievable pretence that Ann's body could have lain there for the best part of three whole days without anyone seeing it. Her body was not seen by anyone because it was not, for most of that period, actually in the field at all. In any case, Ann had not been killed in the roadside scrubland or anywhere near it. The length of exposure of her body to the elements was long enough to permit fly larvae to begin to infect portions of her flesh but the process would have been much more advanced had her body lain exposed for the entire period claimed by the prosecution when Moundis was brought to trial.

It is a common feature of murder cases that people write to the police and relatives laying false claim to vital new information. Edward Chapman and I have received plenty of letters like that, but the one a young Greek studying in England posted to the Chapman family deserves more than cursory scrutiny. The letter, signed and despatched from an address in Stoke-on-Trent, was received five years after Ann's death, at the time when Edward Chapman's demands for a new inquiry focused fresh attention on the affair. In some detail, the letter set out the story of how two workmen, both named, employed by the Greek water authority came across a grey Volkswagen, containing the corpse of a woman slumped across the back seat. The writer went on: 'Being afraid to investigate they went to do what they had to do in a nearby place and on their way back ... they saw the same car, parked in the fields by the street, at the place where the body was found.' The workmen later saw pictures of Ann in the newspapers and recognized her as the woman they had seen in the car. They did not go to the police because they believed nothing but trouble would follow by getting involved in a potentially dangerous business. Edward Chapman's correspondent thought much the same, even five years after Ann's death and two years after the collapse of the junta. He did not want his name mentioned to anybody 'because I think the political situation in Greece has not changed much'. Perhaps this was nothing more than yet another of the red herrings scattered across the trail; but there are enough significant points in the letter to warrant serious attention. First, the letter contains names, easily checked; and second, it would indeed be possible to get a car to or very near the spot – using the mud track at the rear of the field – where Ann's body was found. The implication is that the events described by the two workmen occurred on a working day, a Monday, the day she was discovered. The body had to be transferred to the site chosen for its discovery and a car would be the only practical means of doing this. But, for the investigating authorities, suggestions of this kind posed a serious problem – none of them would fit the trial and conviction of Moundis. And, like everything else which could not be used to throw blame on him, it was rejected at all the appeal hearings.

The contortion of evidence commenced from the moment that Ann's partially-clothed body, lying face down in the scrub with wrists and ankles secured with wire, was discovered by an elderly couple on Monday, 18 October. Being good citizens, they immediately informed the police.

7 · The White House Factor

And now you arrive by some unfair expedient, having neglected,
no doubt, to pay proper attention to the view

— Michael Roberts

Although few Greeks are aware of it, Saturday 16 October
1971 is one of the most significant dates in the history of their
country. On that day, the representative of the most powerful
nation on earth came to address specific demands to a re-
gional, client state and to remind the leadership of that state
of its strictly limited room for manoeuvre. Spiro T. Agnew,
Vice-President of the United States of America, arrived at
Athens airport at lunchtime that Saturday, carrying with
him a precise political shopping list. His objectives were
presidential and beyond the control of Congress, which had
already begun to differ widely with the American administration on policy towards Greece and Cyprus.

Early in 1971, Congress and the White House had em-
barked upon a collision course. The House Foreign Affairs
Committee ordered a series of hearings in March to analyse
what the American government was doing in any objective
manner to lead Greece back towards democracy. Most of
the discussion concentrated on the need to defend NATO
interests in the region while at the same time edging Greece
towards some type of representative government. Rodger
Davies, the senior official at the US Defense Department

BLOOD ON THEIR HANDS

responsible for the evolution of this policy, made two important statements to the committee hearings in July, but these
served only to confirm the suspicions of powerful critics like
Senator William Fulbright that the administration was – and
had been for a long time – playing a double game. Rodger
Davies, whose role in Cyprus would cost him his life, told
the hearings that the problem was how to reconcile NATO
interests in the eastern Mediterranean with a return to Greek
democracy as the best guarantee for stability in the region.
The Colonels had recently unwrapped a package of cosmetic
'reforms' designed to show the world – and in particular to
influence sensitive US opinion – that Greece was already on
the road to constitutional propriety. Rodger Davies spoke of
the administration's delight at these moves which, he said,
showed that 'our influence in Greece could be used in the
most effective manner if we maintained our working relationship with this regime'. Fulbright and others were not impressed. He had already roasted the administration for a
record of actions 'so sympathetic to the Greek Colonels that
it lends very little credence to your declaration that you
are opposed to them . . .' Put another way, Fulbright was
accusing the administration of furtively pursuing strategic
objectives in the region by a covert policy of friendly co-
operation with, and manipulation of, the junta. An embargo
imposed on the supply of military aid was widely acknow-
ledged to have been openly breached by the Americans, both
to reassure the Greek government that a policy of parity with
Turkey would be maintained, and also to make it plain to the
USSR that whatever the White House might say in public,
strategic interests in the region overwhelmed any other political consideration. Late in 1970, even this flimsy pretext was
abandoned and the State Department announced the resump-
tion of normal arms shipments to Greece. Nixon's man on
the spot in Athens, Ambassador Henry Tasca, was still,
one year later in August 1971, offering muddled replies to

ABOVE LEFT: The girl with stars in her eyes: Ann Chapman at the age of two. Growing up, she would delight her parents with hard work at school.

ABOVE: Ann won a place at Manchester University and gained a good degree in psychology. But after leaving university she found it hard to settle down to a fixed career.

BELOW LEFT: She even contemplated a part-time income from working as a model. This Thames-side snap was posed by a photographer friend shortly before she found a way into journalism through Radio London.

A girl who cared about her appearance sufficiently to undergo cosmetic surgery to alter the shape of her nose. This was Ann's passport photograph, the one released to the press after her body was found near the Pine Hill Hotel. It offers a considerable contrast to post-operation portraits, like the one (*below*) taken a short time before she left for Greece.

OPPOSITE ABOVE: The Greek jottings made by Gareth Davies in Ann's diary weeks before she left on her journey to death. Investigators believed, wrongly, that they represented a secret code. They were merely attempts to impress by a slightly pompous young doctor to whom Ann had revealed her fascination for Greece.

OPPOSITE BELOW: But there is an important message in Ann's diary doodlings (far right). She was making active preparations for the Greek journey. The key phrase is 'Find name of Fiat garage'. In Corfu she hired a car at a pre-arranged garage to make an 80 kilometre journey, almost certainly to meet a contact and receive instructions.

Sunday 2nd after Epiphany
17

Gareth ap A G James

Monday
18

a b c d e f g h i
j k l m n o p q r s t u v
w x y z.

Tuesday
19

abcdefghijklmnopqrstuvwxz

Wednesday
20

Thursday
21

As I was
young and easy under
the apple boughs about
the

Friday
22

μεῖζονα ἀγάπην
οὐδεὶς ἔχει ἵνα
τις τὴν ψυχὴν
αὐτοῦ τῆς ἑαυτοῦ

ἵνα Blunted

Sunday 17th after Trinity
3 Teachers Against Racism
Teach In on Racism - Conway Hall
10 - 4

Monday
4 0 Phone about Steptoe reception
Dateline

1.30.
5.00 Interview Manzys.

Tuesday
5 Prof. Terence Morris.
women + crime.

Wednesday
6 Sean Tulin G.C.
phone afternoon

7.00 244 Alexandra Park Rd.
N. 22
Wood Green cab W.3. end ?

870 1451
£1 · 03p. cld.
20th Sept £1 · 25
Thursday
7

12.00 Steptoe reception

7.00. 244 Alexandra Rd. N.22
Wood Green cab W.3 end Rd.
Bikini, Greek money, batteries, adapter,
cassette
Fond name of Fiat Garage
News info. 1) Greece - tourism arts
culture traditions
2) Women in prison

Friday
8

Mike Sparrow L.N.L. ½

Saturday
9

Olympics 727 8050
Elizabeth
U.F.T.A. Conference

ABOVE: The Pine Hill Hotel in Kavouri, where A⬛
was last seen alive by Nicholas Clarkson, one of t⬛
travel agents touring Greece with the Olympic
Holidays party.

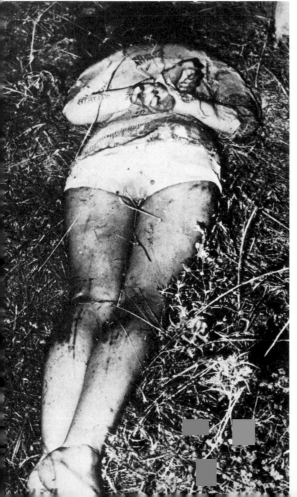

LEFT: Ann's body as it was found by an elderly
couple searching for edible snails. Both the first
police officer on the scene and Dr Kapsaskis, the
forensic scientist, were puzzled by the lack of any
signs of a struggle. Her wrists and ankles (close-u⬛
have been secured by wire, the knots facing
outwards. The experts concluded it would need t⬛
people to move her body and tie her up in this
manner.

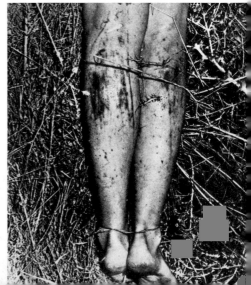

ABOVE: At the beginning of his long search for justice: Ann's father, the redoubtable Edward Chapman, pictured at the trial which sentenced Nicholas Moundis to life imprisonment for his daughter's manslaughter. But Edward Chapman left the courtroom convinced there had been a political cover-up.

LEFT: Moundis, the former prison guard framed for the killing of Ann Chapman, being marched into the Athens courtroom. By this time he had already recanted his confession.

Pictures at an exhibition. Moundis, during a thoroughly rehearsed re-enactment of his alleged crime, describes to court officers and journalists how he found Ann sitting on a low wall waiting for a bus.

According to the confession he swiftly retracted, Ann at first willingly climbed over the wall with him for a sexual adventure.

But when Ann saw his wedding ring, she began to resist. They struggled on a patch of wasteland not far from the bus stop.

After strangling or suffocating his victim – Moundis was never sure which – he dragged her body away. A plainclothes policeman stands in for the body. But the autopsy proved that Ann's corpse could never have been moved in this way.

ABOVE: The wife's tale. Mrs Moundis denounces her husband to the packed court. Moundis (top right, second row, centre) watches in disbelief.

LEFT: And then the evidence of his wife's aunt, Katherine Molion: she too quarrelled with Moundis before denouncing him to the Athens police.

questions as to exactly when that decision had actually been taken; this evasion was necessary to conceal the fact that the embargo had never actually existed. Other key figures popped up in the Greek capital offering support and encouragement. The US Defense Secretary, Malcolm Laird, was there in October 1970, his visit marred by an explosion in the very building where he was in conference with Papadopoulos. The British Defence Minister, Lord Carrington, went to Greece, ostensibly 'on holiday', but no one believed that assurance from London.

Since the Colonels were proving so compliant – though not yet shifting significant ground over Cyprus – Nixon and his advisers were confident that they could deal with any trouble in Congress. But September proved a dangerous month in the Mediterranean and, as events throughout the whole region began to threaten a disintegration of the existing fragile stability, the need for tougher and more precise objectives became more pressing with each passing day. Turkey, the other NATO power in the area, was slipping into political chaos which would eventually lead to an army coup in Ankara. Libya had fallen to a Muslim fanatic, Colonel Gaddafi. In Egypt, Nasser died and King Hussein's 'Black Friday' attack on PLO guerrillas in Jordan posed the threat of a Middle East war, forestalled in the event only by the timely appearance of the US Sixth Fleet. Despite political strains inside the Greek military junta, the situation in Greece appeared serene compared to developing unrest elsewhere. A decision was taken in the White House that humanitarian heart-bleeding over the internal political situation in Greece was superfluous political baggage to be thrown overboard as the weather roughened; more than that, the Americans worried that Cyprus contained all the combustible ingredients for a major explosion which could destroy all that was left of political stability in the area.

Nixon gave orders for a major change in policy. American

VIPs visiting Greece as official couriers were encouraged to make glowing remarks at public banquets about the achievement of economic and political stability in the country – an astonishing indication of how the US had determined to back the Colonels, at a price, of course. No one doubted that Nixon and, equally significantly, his Greek-American Vice-President, Spiro Agnew, were crafting the design inside the White House. Far from enjoying an 'economic miracle', as those proconsuls despatched by Nixon eagerly prattled to all they met, the Greek economy was stagnating and the Colonels had no idea what to do about it, except somehow cling to power. But the flattery the Colonels received from the other side of the Atlantic earned them the huge political bonus of posing before the people of Greece as trustworthy guardians of the nation. No one in the junta was particularly disturbed by the formation of the National Resistance Council to co-ordinate opposition outside the country, since nearly all resistance activity so far had proved little more than a minor irritant and easy to contain, thanks to a helping hand from friendly foreign intelligence agencies. It is true that Nixon appreciated the risks of completely isolating himself from Congress. And so Tasca was despatched upon a European tour to meet all the leading exiles, including the deposed Constantine and Karamanlis. It is hard to believe later protestations from the Colonels that they were completely in ignorance of these contacts, which led to a suitably dramatic and obviously stage-managed rebuke to the Americans from the Athens government, and, as a penalty, a temporary halt to the development of shore facilities for the US Navy in Greece. In retrospect, the affair looks contrived rather than a botch; but it continues to be the source of historic embarrassment to Karamanlis and Constantine, whom suspicious minds in Greece remain convinced were both party to secret briefings by Tasca on the future course of American policy, particularly towards Cyprus. After this brave gesture of defiance by Papadopoulos, he got on with the more important business of listening to the overtures of American negotiators.

The need for a secure base for the Sixth Fleet had become acute after another political eruption in the Mediterranean brought the flamboyant Don Mintoff and his Labour government to power in Malta: both were determined to evict NATO vessels from their Valetta base. On 13 March, the Turkish army ended civilian rule in Ankara, bringing closer, to American eyes, the possibility of fresh disturbances in Cyprus which might well threaten a Mediterranean war engulfing two NATO powers, Greece and Turkey. Gaddafi had already served notice to quit upon the American naval bases in Libya. A new home for the fleet was now a crucial necessity, as was action to prevent a war in Cyprus. On both fronts, the junta now commenced active discussions with the Americans. In the summer of 1971, Papadopoulos sent what he thought was a clandestine warning to Archbishop Makarios, threatening that harsh measures would follow unless the Greek Cypriots respected the wishes of the 'national centre' in Athens. The contents of this message, clearly hinting at the necessity for partition, were revealed to the world by the German news magazine *Der Spiegel*, together with an abrupt and dismissive reply from Makarios. Without doubt, Makarios arranged the leak personally.

By the time Spiro Agnew arrived in Athens, relationships between Athens and Nicosia had plunged to their lowest point for years. Makarios suspected the junta in Athens of nurturing plots to eliminate him in order to remove the most significant obstacle to the imposition of partition through the willing participation of the two military governments in Greece and Turkey. Professor Nicholas Devlotoglou has suggested that secret contact had been established between the exiled Karamanlis and Bulent Ecevit, the Turkish social democrat premier who fled Ankara when the army took power, and that Cyprus was the key element in their discussions. The Turks had always maintained emergency plans to intervene in Cyprus, which foresaw the annexation of approximately one-third of the island. This could easily accommodate the Turkish Cypriot population. The overwhelming military superiority of Turkey over Greece was a significant factor in the decades of rivalry between the two countries but, nevertheless, Turkey would always require some kind of pretext for intervention in Cyprus. As events would prove, such a pretext could be found.

The first steps towards it were taken in 1971 when the old anti-British guerrilla leader, General Grivas, suddenly vanished from his retirement home in Athens. Grivas was sent back to Cyprus by Papadopoulos to establish a fresh bridgehead in the form of a military force aimed at challenging the rule of Makarios. Grivas, who always preferred old and well-tried tricks to new ones, created a movement known as EOKA–B. Makarios responded by setting up a new force under his own personal control, the reserve guard. The Archbishop had no faith in the official Cypriot military force, the National Guard, because it was staffed and openly under the control of Athens. Grivas went to Cyprus as an unreformed Hellenist, having been briefed by Papadopoulos to prepare for a final and inevitable assault which would at last set the 'jewel in the crown'. An ageing veteran of countless battles against the British, Grivas had not suspected the deceit that lay behind Papadopoulos' command. Nor did Ioannides, when the moment came for him to order an insurrection perfectly designed to inspire Turkish intervention. The extent of contact between the military regimes in Athens and Ankara can never be precisely determined; but the desire of both to survive and enjoy the continuing support of their American benefactors cannot be underestimated. The price of survival was a solution in Cyprus, where the bitter enmities aroused since independence increasingly pointed to the need for separation of the two communities. By exploiting mutual distrust and suspicion between the Greeks and Turks – in essence by promising both sides something of what they most wanted in Cyprus – the Americans saw the opportunity for a highly satisfactory solution. They could be absolutely sure of the willing compliance of a British government deeply concerned with the maintenance of its own sovereign bases in Cyprus, especially after the Mintoff victory in Malta, which indicated a painful closure of British (and therefore NATO) bases on the George Cross island.

However, not everyone inside the junta's ring of power in Athens was entirely content at the prospect of a sell-out in Cyprus in order to please the Americans and, much less, the Turks. The regent, Zoitakis, who was theoretically keeping the throne warm for Constantine, enraged Papadopoulos by openly opposing any attempt to oust Makarios. Brooding in his eyrie at the ESA headquarters, Ioannides watched the turn of events with contentment, convinced that the contortions performed by Papadopoulos to keep himself in power would soon open the way for a coup-within-a-coup.

Ambassador Tasca's first job as he hurried Spiro Agnew from Athens airport to a formal state encounter with Papadopoulos on 16 October was to assure the Vice-President that the situation was entirely under control. Agnew had eight days in which to make his message plain to the Colonels. This was: we will maintain control of international public opinion providing a base for the Sixth Fleet is rapidly and effectively established and progress is made towards a division of the two communities in Cyprus. Agnew was welcomed by a trio of junta leaders, Papadopoulos, Makarezos and the chief of the armed forces, Angelis, all of them keen to derive the maximum personal and political benefit from the arrival of the most distinguished VIP to enter the country since the seizure of power. Later that day there were private talks between Agnew and Papadopoulos, with Tasca in attendance, and in the evening a full-scale state dinner with almost every luminary of the junta on hand. These theatricals had all the cosmetic elements of a public relations success, except for the embarrassment caused by a series of small bomb explosions in the area near the airport (and Ann Chapman's hotel at Kavouri). These were organized by a retired and much-decorated air force officer, Tassos Minis, and the explosives were supplied by the resistance operating overland from Europe. Minis and two accomplices paid for this outrage with prolonged brutal interrogation and torture and more than a hundred days in solitary confinement. The trivial damage caused by the blast was a much lesser offence than embarrassment caused to the regime.

After sightseeing and relaxing on Sunday, the Vice-President spent Monday talking to armed forces chiefs and communing with Papadopoulos, usually with Tasca in attendance. Tuesday saw him talking again with the armed forces leaders before setting off on an exercise designed to shore up the image of Papadopoulos as the saviour of Greece. His home in the village of Garaglianoi was undergoing political consecration as a national shrine. Agnew played the role perfectly, even down to the obligatory lunch in a taverna with the local mayor, before setting off by helicopter to Crete, the island which Ann Chapman had been due to visit at precisely the same time. From there he flew on to Rhodes, but at this point the schedule was interrupted by Agnew's sudden return to Athens. The Colonels' propaganda-managers blamed the weather – although, by all accounts, there was nothing sufficiently threatening in the Aegean to explain Agnew's abrupt change of plan. Agnew had, in fact, returned to Athens in the company of Tasca because of thunderstorms affecting the political climate. He reported to his general satisfaction that home port facilities for the Sixth Fleet seemed assured, but also indicated that serious resistance was developing inside the junta to partition as a solution in Cyprus. Papadopoulos had appreciated, perhaps for the first time, that he had over-reached himself by conniving at American plans – later to be demonstrated in a mini-coup in which he ousted the doubting Zoitakis, principal opponent of US intrigue over Cyprus, and assumed the regency himself.

Agnew flew back to Washington on Saturday 23 October, his mission largely but not entirely accomplished. The regime had been able to demonstrate the face of acceptable government to a powerful military and political ally, and thus to the world, and had also bought time to comply with the full extent of American requirements in Cyprus. This period of tranquillity was not to last for long. The 'BBC reporter', Ann Chapman, had been murdered in the capital on the night before Agnew's arrival. The order went out for a full-scale cover-up to avoid any compromising connection with the government or its security forces, although both were thoroughly implicated. The Lady Fleming affair had also aroused an international sensation. She had been involved in an attempt to free Panagoulis, the man who had so narrowly failed to assassinate Papadopoulos. After being given a sixteen-month gaol sentence, Amelia Fleming was suddenly released and deported to Britain on 21 October, a few days after Ann's body was found. Lady Fleming's name and her connection with the man who came within a hair's-breadth of killing the senior dictator gave the resistance movement a much-needed injection of encouragement. Both events, if a connection was made between them, would give the lie to the junta's boasts about internal security and the enduring affection of the Greek people. The Colonels responded by rounding up a pair of active communist resistance leaders who had secretly returned to the country, thus providing convenient, if mostly coincidental, proof for their claims about the 'communist threat within'.

The outcome of the Agnew visit had not pleased Ioannides,

who was biding his time less than patiently, ready to seize power at the first sign of weakness by Papadopoulos. An interesting example of this impatience comes from the Athens lawyer and former Euro MP, Costas Gontikas, who from April to December 1971 was representing the manager of the Athens office of American Express Travel, Dimitri Papaefstratiou. The latter had been arrested on suspicion of aiding the resistance. This was true. The American Express premises were used as an underground post office where messages and money, mostly for relatives of victims of the regime, could be left. Papaefstratiou was eventually picked up by an ESA squad and held in solitary confinement at the Greek gestapo's headquarters, not far from the Hilton Hotel. On several occasions Gontikas was allowed to see his client, who was held under what he described as 'severe psychological distress' in a very small cell. During one of these visits, Gontikas, who understood Ioannides' reputation only too well, was surprised and perturbed to be invited into his office and lectured on the misfortunes of Greece under the Papadopoulos regime. Ioannides went through each member of the government listing their faults, reserving the largest amount of scorn for Papadopoulos. Gontikas was therefore not surprised when Ioannides finally seized power.

The arrest of the manager of the leading American tourist bureau in Athens led to widespread political ructions which extended all the way back to Washington. It is a measure of Ioannides' confidence and independence that he was capable of defying Papadopoulos, who had been instructed by the Americans in no uncertain terms to 'get the man out'. There is also a direct connection with Ann Chapman. Her notebook contains the name of a contact at the American Express travel office in London. Although attempts to trace that contact have failed, it is clear that Ann's knowledge of the resistance movement was deep enough to reveal the significance of the

94

American Express office in Athens and the unusual facilities offered there.

The reverberations of the Agnew visit of 16 October 1971 continue to this day. From exile in Europe, Andreas Papandreou's well-displayed antennae – manipulated to a certain extent by the CIA – intercepted intelligence concerning American intentions in Cyprus and Tasca's discussions with exiled political leaders, including his deeply resented rival, Karamanlis, who received similar signals. The reaction of both was to let the Americans go ahead with escorting the junta towards such a monumental folly, since the subsequent turmoil would be certain to sweep the junta from power and open the way, as each saw it, for the realization of his own political ambitions. But when the Colonels did fall in the wake of the Cyprus tragedy, it was Karamanlis and not Papandreou who received the summons to head a government of national unity and lead the way back to democracy. Andreas Papandreou has never forgiven the Americans for what he believes to be an act of political treason against him. The US bases, the seed of Agnew's visit in October 1971, remain to this day a perpetually flowering reminder of how his own struggle for power was subverted by the Americans. He was also severely stung by the accusation that he had allowed himself to be manipulated, unwittingly or otherwise, by the CIA. A policy cornerstone of his eccentric administration, which has betrayed virtually every promise it has made to the Greek electorate, is to rid Greece of the American bases. An agreement to roughly that effect was reached in 1983, but it remains, at the time of writing, subject to differing interpretations by both sides. Relationships between Greece and the USA have remained consistently poor throughout Papandreou's years in power, rarely rising above frosty, and occasionally plunging below zero over incidents like the hijacking of a TWA airliner by terrorists at Athens airport. Papandreou employs all his political craft, much of it learnt from his father, to stay in power by using the old trick of distracting public opinion whenever the government faces severe internal stress. By the end of 1985, Greece had been overwhelmed by an avalanche of economic problems, leading to the imposition of a draconian austerity regime which sparked off a wave of strikes and severe political ruptures inside PASOK. Papandreou responded by sending 200,000 demonstrators to the gates of the American embassy, including the disturbing innovation of conscripts in military uniform, to demand closure of the bases. On that night, the anniversary of the polytechnic students' revolt against the Colonels in 1973, a fifteen-year-old boy was shot by police after hurling, it was alleged, a Molotov cocktail at a police car. The cycle of death, drama and destruction which has been the enduring feature of Greece in every decade since independence, had begun to assert itself once again.

8 · Fragments of Deception

The wicked is snared in the work of his own hands.

— Psalm 9

The last light of day was fading quickly on the evening of 18 October as an elderly couple made their way along the narrow rough track which bordered the patch of scrub ground near the bus stop at St Nicholas. George Hatzijannis, later described in police records as a 'poor builder', and his wife were searching along the tumbling stone wall for a well-known local delicacy – small, edible snails. They had used the track many times before and knew the area intimately. Little was likely to disturb their foray, since the track served only a few isolated houses and the field below it was rarely, if ever, used for grazing. Later Hatzijannis told the police that his attention was attracted by a few coloured scraps of clothing near a crop of low bushes. He climbed over the dry-stone wall to encounter the body of a young woman lying face down, her hands and feet tied with wire and her face battered. Hatzijannis fled the scene to telephone the police. What happened during these moments is of paramount significance to all subsequent attempts to excavate the truth.

In any efficiently conducted police operation, the person who finds the body is a key witness for the defence or the prosecution. Hatzijannis, however, was discarded as a trivial participant who had little more than circumstantial evidence to offer. It is true that Hatzijannis did not hang around the scene to make a detailed investigation – he was too frightened; but over the years he has remained consistent in his description of exactly how Ann lay, what she was wearing and, significantly, despite all the later claims, the absence of stones covering the body. It was later suggested that stones had been taken from the wall over which Hatzijannis had climbed and had been stacked upon various parts of the body. This story emerges in both the forensic report contributed by Dr Dimitrios Kapsaskis and the report of the first police officer to arrive on the scene. Hatzijannis has stuck to his story over the years: he did not see any stones on the body. The claim that an extraordinarily large stone (about the weight of the average adult male) had been propped upon Ann's right cheek and another about half that size on her forearm, was later seized upon by Moundis' prosecutors to obscure the fact that the body had been moved at some point between the time of actual death and the discovery of the corpse. This vital fact would have prevented Moundis' conviction. The forensic surgeon, Dr Kapsaskis, used the stones when Moundis was brought for trial to explain certain discolorations on Ann's body, the condition known as hypostasis. The longer a body lies untouched, the more pronounced this condition becomes: blood gathers naturally in the direction that the corpse faces, appearing as a purplish-blue lividity of the flesh, similar to extensive bruising. Hypostasis had formed on both the front and back of Ann's body, suggesting to Dr Kapsaskis that she had been moved from one position to another at a considerable period after death. He was later to claim – flying in the face of all the findings in his own post-mortem report – that Ann's body had never been moved at all, but that instead the heavy stones found stacked upon the corpse somehow accounted for the condition of hypostasis on the back of the body. This conveniently removed the proposition that she had been moved after death. But Hatzijannis said nothing to the police about stones. He was questioned at Vouliagmeni police station shortly after reporting the discovery of the body, but never at any other time. He was never summoned to give evidence at the trial, despite the insistence of Edward Chapman, or at any of the subsequent re-examinations of the case. The police never disturbed him again, but one independent investigator did.

In the years which followed the collapse of the junta, Moundis was fighting to prove his innocence and Edward Chapman was in rapid pursuit of a state-inspired cover-up of the death of his daughter. George Trangas, an intelligent and capable young journalist working for the Athens daily newspaper *Vraydini*, was puzzled by almost every aspect of the Chapman case and began reworking the ground from scratch. He started with Hatzijannis and his wife, talking to them at length, getting the husband to describe into a tape-recorder exactly what he had seen in the field at Vouliagmeni on the evening of 18 October. Hatzijannis never faltered in his story. He saw no stones. Trangas revealed this and much more in his newspaper. The authorities ignored him. So he went one stage further and actively intervened on the side of Moundis and the Chapmans. Trangas turned his tape-recordings of Hatzijannis over to officials of the court who were re-examining the evidence against Moundis. According to the records of the court, they were later strangely mislaid and then lost completely. In short, a conspiracy which had commenced in the climate of a military dictatorship spilled over into the so-called democratic years. Two different political administrations, the 'New Conservatives' under Karamanlis and the socialist governments of Andreas Papandreou – neither of whom had anything obvious to gain from hiding the misdeeds of the Colonels or their henchmen – permitted interference with vital evidence to continue.

To allow even the slightest element of doubt over the significance of the stones could light a fuse which might well blow apart the case against Moundis. Perhaps Hatzijannis, in the panic of the moment, had overlooked the stones – though this would be surprising since the record suggested that one was at least as heavy as a man; perhaps the police photographer called to the scene asked for these large objects to be moved before he could commence his work – an astonishing interference with material evidence. The corpse was photographed from almost every angle. There are no signs of stones on or anywhere near it. It can be suggested that the finding of the body was in itself premature, since the longer Ann remained exposed to the elements, the faster the process of decomposition would camouflage important forensic clues. This process was advancing but had not reached the point at which it could prevent Dr Kapsaskis – at this stage innocent of implication in a wider conspiracy – from producing a thorough post-mortem report.

Kapsaskis arrived quickly at the scene, having been summoned in the wake of a force of gendarmerie officers commanded by Captain Theodore Tsoutsias. Tsoutsias' official deposition records that approximately an hour after discovery of the body was reported to the Vouliagmeni police station by Hatzijannis – that was at about 5.30 p.m. – he led a large force of officers to the scene, including the director of the gendarmerie's criminal investigation services, Lieutenant Colonel Basil Papadakos, and a photographer. Tsoutsias described the corpse as covered with dry grasses and thistles, the hands and ankles tied with wire, the knots facing outwards. Stones were disposed upon the body against the right cheek and lying across the forearm. The body, still unidentified, was lightly clothed: a coloured blouse, torn on the left sleeve and the right shoulder, and a pair of underpants, stained with a small amount of blood in the genital area and indicating, as Tsoutsias recorded, menstruation taking place before death. The prosecution claimed at Moundis' trial that he killed Ann in a fit of sexual passion, after attempting to interfere with her genitals. But Captain Tsoutsias was positive that the pants were in 'a normal position' and there were no indications of any attempt to remove them. He saw, in the fading light of an overcast evening, an opening in a wire fence to the east of the site, and concluded that her wrists and ankles had been secured with wire cut from the fence. The small force of gendarmerie officers spread out over the site but 'because of the advancing night' it was decided to postpone a thorough search until daylight. Dr Kapsaskis had meanwhile arrived and made what he could of the scene from the headlights of a police car. His preliminary diagnosis, advanced to Tsoutsias for entry into the official record, described the body of a young woman who had been killed about forty-eight hours previously. Death was due to strangulation. Certain injuries apparent on the body had been inflicted while she was still alive and her wrists and ankles had been secured with wire after death. Kapsaskis ordered removal of the body to the city mortuary for post-mortem examination and Tsoutsias gave instructions for the search of the site to start again at first light.

Kapsaskis had a long history as a compliant servant of successive regimes, and his record throughout the period of the Colonels is stained by the abuse of his considerable professional skills in the service of the state. But on this occasion Kapsaskis went home to his Athens flat to ponder what appeared to be a straightforward case of murder, uncomplicated in the sense that he could apparently set to work without any necessity to compromise the evidence. The thoroughness with which he commenced his work the following day, assisted by his deputy, George Ayoutantis, is a testimony to professional expertise. Like Captain Tsoutsias, he also established that Ann's underpants had not been disturbed in any way — the first of many serious conflicts with the subsequent evidence against Moundis, who later described in his retracted confession his attempts to touch her genitals and his discovery that she was menstruating – though he was confused as to whether he encountered a sanitary towel or an internal tampon (it was, in fact, a tampon). Decomposition of the corpse was revealed by bluish-green patching on the lower abdomen. Infestation by flies had set in and some eggs had hatched in the flesh. Kapsaskis noted accurately the condition of hypostasis well advanced on the frontal trunk of the body and on the thighs, in accordance with the position in which she was found, lying face down. But, far more revealingly, hypostasis had also set in on the right shoulder, on the upper back and the right side of the thorax – absolute proof that the body had originally lain for some time on its back before being turned over. Kapsaskis, pursuing his work with diligence, did not restrain his diagnosis: the differing positions of the tell-tale hypostasis condition supplied absolute proof that the body had been moved after death. To leave no room for doubt, he noted all the other crucial signs: a yellowish tinge on the left cheek 'due to friction with a rough surface'; a dark mark extending from the chin, under the jaw, across the throat to the left ear 'due to detachment of the epidermis during friction with a smooth surface such as a wide strip of cloth'; friction marks from the strap of the brassiere across the left breast; linear strip marks along the back of the lower thighs, the hollows of the knees and calves, on both legs, 'caused by friction with the edge of a firm object' or, in non-forensic language, some kind of material such as a strap or a piece of clothing which could be used to transport a body. Kapsaskis summed all this up as follows:

> The presence of the paler hypostasis on the right shoulder and the side and back of the thorax in contrast to the fully-established hypostasis on the front of the body can only be explained by a change in the position of the body before the elapse of seven hours from death when hypostasis becomes permanent. The body must have

been moved not earlier than one and a half hours after death, when hypostasis in the case of death from asphyxia first appears. The theory that the body was moved is also borne out by the parchment-like marks, such as that made by the brassiere . . . moreover, the tying of the hands and feet after death and the presence of a parchment-like mark made by the wire used for this purpose indicates friction with the wire during movement.

If the body had been dragged instead of carried about, as the prosecution against Moundis would allege, there should have been some revealing marks, like scratching or bruising on all likely points of contact with the ground, such as the heels, feet or shoulders. Kapsaskis noted there were no such marks, 'so it is unlikely that the body was dragged by the hands or feet while being moved'. To move Ann's body in the manner which the autopsy suggests, at least two individuals would have been necessary. Again, the timing which would fit the Moundis conviction is hopelessly wrong. From evidence which was never contradicted – from his father-in-law who picked him up in his own taxi – Moundis was many kilometres away from the field at St Nicholas at the time when he was supposed to be indulging in athletic exercises with a corpse. The prosecution's reconstruction of these events has Moundis toiling about the murder scene, hauling the corpse around and concealing it with large and heavy stones, stopping to clip or break wire from a fence (at night, with no light or means of cutting the wire to help him) and securing the wrists and ankles in a complicated fashion for no apparent reason. Dead bodies do not struggle.

Before his trial, Moundis took part in a series of re-enactments of his alleged crime, all of which he later denounced as theatrical episodes thoroughly and privately rehearsed under the tuition of the police officers who arrested

103

and accused him. The official photographs of the reconstruction depict Moundis tying the ankles in such a way that the knot faced outwards. He demonstrated tying the wrists in the same manner. Yet this could only be achieved by turning the body over and returning it to a prone position or by seating it on a chair, so that the knot is in the right direction, facing outwards, when the corpse is in the prone position. In the second instance, the assistance of a second individual would have been essential. During the trial, much was made of Moundis' semi-literacy and his past behaviour as a voyeur. He had been in trouble with the police sufficiently often to realize, if he really was the killer, that bolting well clear of the scene was the wisest course of action. The events which took place in the field at St Nicholas were calculated with a precision of mind which Moundis did not possess.

By the time Dr Kapsaskis had begun his work so methodically in the mortuary, he altered his original estimate about the time of death, setting this back from forty-eight to a more probable seventy-two hours before the actual discovery of the body. He established this from the stage of development of the insect larvae which had begun to hatch in the flesh, and also from the progress of digestion of the small quantity of food found in the stomach. Kapsaskis considered that a small meal had been consumed about an hour before death, a snack such as a sandwich 'about the size of a small fist'. Yet everyone agrees that Ann had not eaten during the last day of her life. Nothing in the conviction of Moundis permits even a moment for food. So now we have the extraordinary proposition that food somehow found its way into her stomach after she died. A further vital clue was advanced by the condition of the tampon within her vagina. The amount of absorption suggested that it had been changed about two, and certainly not more than six, hours before death, which is entirely consistent with her wash and brush-up at the Pine Hill Hotel. Kapsaskis concluded: 'Death must therefore have occurred approximately during the night of the 15th to the 16th of the month, about an hour after food was taken and a few hours after the tampon was changed.'

Kapsaskis was in no doubt that strangulation was the cause of death. He noted a fractured rib and considered that this had been caused by the downward pressure of a knee. Bruise marks caused by fingers on the throat could be clearly seen, the result of strangulation applied with such force that Ann began to inhale blood from her nose and pharynx – as Kapsaskis put it, 'during the violent constriction of the neck by means of the hand'. He was equally conclusive about the injuries to her head. There were multiple bruises and abrasions on the centre and right of the forehead and across the bridge of the nose and around the left eye – 'all caused by a blunt instrument'. Similar bruises repeated themselves on both arms, and across her back. All this was consistent with a severe roughing-up before death. Kapsaskis thought so too: but he actually went further and chillingly indicated the manner of her death, drawing on a lifetime dealing with the gory business of murder. He wrote: 'The bruises on either side of the arms are marks made by fingers of hands which violently grasped the person by the arms in order to immobilize her, probably from behind as indicated by the position of the thumb marks on the backs of the arms.' Kapsaskis saw what had happened as though he had actually been present. One individual grasped Ann firmly by the arms from the rear, almost certainly while she was seated: the second strangled her with a terrifying grip. No matter how much this evidence is twisted and distorted, it cannot fit the explanation of murder by a single individual. The autopsy also proves that Ann was beaten into submission, perhaps to the point of unconsciousness. Kapsaskis had no doubts about that either. His report is concluded in these terms: 'Strangulation was preceded by ill treatment liable to lessen the power of resistance. Death must have occurred during the night of 15 to 16 October. The body was moved to the place where it was found.' The significance of that key statement was never examined by any court in Greece and neither were Kapsaskis or Ayoutantis ever cross-examined on their crucial conclusion that Ann had not been killed in the place where her body was discovered. Quite obviously, such an admission would have precipitated the collapse of the case against Moundis. The autopsy report is absolutely silent on the business of large boulders supposedly stacked upon the corpse causing all the marks and bruises found on the head and arms. Instead, Kapsaskis was quite certain that these contusions were caused by a severe beating before death and subsequent movement of the corpse. He never invested the stones, if they ever really existed, with any significance until it became necessary to create the fiction that Moundis was the killer. During all the years of deliberate distortion, the report signed by Kapsaskis and his deputy Ayoutantis shines upon the truth like the beam from a powerful torch.

9 · Beacons on the Trail

O what a tangled web we weave,
When first we practise to deceive!

— Sir Walter Scott

The few early risers travelling along the main Athens to
Sounion highway on the cold, damp morning of 19 October
would not have been able to ignore the heavy police activity
around Kavouri and, in particular, at the St Nicholas bus
stop. Police vehicles lined both sides of the road and more
were deployed outside the Pine Hill Hotel. But even the
moderately curious would have merely assumed that the
police were out in force in connection with massive security
for the Agnew visit. The capital had been thronged with
police reinforcements for more than a week and Kavouri's
position near the main airport, from which the US Vice-
President would shortly depart, endowed it with special
strategic significance. The story of the murder of a British
citizen, who also happened to be a reporter with the BBC,
was not yet current except at the highest levels in the police
and gendarmerie headquarters and along the corridors of the
building which housed the security apparatus of the Greek
state. There is evidence of a hurried conference between the
top echelons of KYP and their American controllers, the
CIA, on the evening of the 18th, not long after Hatzijannis'
telephone call alerted the gendarmerie to the discovery of the

unidentified woman in the field at Kavouri. The Americans were concerned lest a scandal break which could easily compromise Agnew's visit. The senior dictator, Papadopoulos, shared this concern. But all this was merely surface pretence over an intelligence operation which had gone disastrously wrong at around midnight on 15 October, when Ann had been strangled to death. Every trace of the panic which followed that event has been expunged from files which even secret service agencies under the control of dictatorships maintain – all, that is, except the dangerous letter which was already on its way to Edward Chapman from the Greek embassy in London, revealing the concern over her fate which had been felt there since Sunday, some twenty-four hours before the actual discovery of the body. The friendly amity between the Greek secret service and their Western partners, the CIA and Britain's MI6, could only be subjected to severe strain by the assassination of a British journalist in a bungled attempt to discover the extent of her knowledge of sensitive policy and, in turn, how much that was known about such matters had leaked to the resistance movement. Throughout the weekend of the murder, those involved in the complicated matrix of the secret Greek state and its interconnected links with the Western intelligence agencies, wrestled with the embarrassing fact of Ann Chapman's death.

The killing of a foreigner, especially a journalist whose activities had attracted the particular attention of the intelligence-gatherers, would be extremely difficult to reveal to public opinion both inside and outside Greece. Complete concealment of the event was obviously futile. At the same time, it was essential to avoid any political overtones and isolate the state from involvement. In these circumstances, only one course of action clearly proposed itself, namely to allow the fact of Ann's death to 'emerge' gradually as a criminal riddle which the gendarmerie and the police would then be permitted to investigate but, despite all efforts, fail to solve. Ann was young and physically attractive and it is part of the Greek folk view of young foreigners visiting their country that many are sexually adventurous. A partly-clothed body found in a field ought to suggest a sexual motive, like attempted rape. The problem was lack of time: the Olympic party staying at the Pine Hill Hotel were already concerned by her disappearance and any one of them might shortly contact the girl's parents or the authorities in Britain. Ann needed to reappear as a corpse, in explicable circumstances, as a matter of urgency. Management of this task was delegated to the lowest level possible, on the basis that the fewer people who knew the facts the better.

At each stage of the operation, however, something went wrong, leaving behind an indelible trail of confusion from which vital clues would later be read. Dr Kapsaskis, the automatic choice to perform the autopsy, was not immediately asked to render his customary services as the perfect forensic camouflage artist. Because Kapsaskis had been kept deliberately in the dark, at least during all the early stages, he – and Captain Tsoutsias – were altogether much too thorough in their work. Both were puzzled by the lack of any obvious signs of the struggle which might reasonably have featured strongly in an encounter between Ann and her killer, or killers. Both Kapsaskis and Tsoutsias quickly perceived the lack of any obvious attempt sexually to abuse the girl, because in the panic which developed after Ann's murder, the significance of her period was entirely overlooked. The point of dumping her in the field at Vouliagmeni, not far from the hotel where she was last seen alive, was to suggest a folly which had gone wrong at that spot. But again, those responsible failed to appreciate how the dead can speak through the medium of forensic reports, and the work of Kapsaskis created enormous difficulties right from the start by revealing the crucial fact that the corpse had been moved.

How this confusion unravelled itself in the days after the

discovery of Ann's body can easily be deduced from the peculiar manner in which the police began the search for clues at the 'murder site'. Just as Ann herself had been moved, her belongings demonstrated a strange ability to materialize at various stages of the search. When Captain Tsoutsias assembled his forces not long after dawn on the 19th, he appeared to be faced with a relatively straightforward task. This was to hunt for clues within an area not much bigger than two good-sized building plots, with easy access and not too much in the way of thick undergrowth to conceal the evidence. Tsoutsias adopted the standard procedure of dividing up the area into two main search sectors. Nevertheless, at the end of the first day, the painstaking inch-by-inch examination of the ground yielded no more than a ring from Ann's finger and three cheap biro pens. There were a few traces of dried blood on the grass corresponding to the position where Ann's left cheek had lain in contact with the ground. The weather during the weekend had included torrential rain, interspersed with warm sunshine. It was curious that such a theoretically thorough forensic investigation at the scene failed to relate these climatic conditions to the possibility of finding blood traces. If the body had lain exposed for a full weekend which included periods of heavy downpour, who could reasonably expect to find traces of blood? Tsoutsias was more puzzled by what he failed to find than by what he did. His report states: 'Both on the spot and all over the extent of the building site, no clear signs of a struggle between the victim and the perpetrators were observed, nor any other evidence to convince one that the victim was executed in the place where it was found.'

At this stage, Tsoutsias is supposed not to have known the identity of the young woman. This dove-tailed with the decision to allow the affair to 'emerge' for exposure as a criminal incident with no compromising links to high places. If Tsoutsias was suspicious, he gave no hint in the early stages of his report, although he had already set down one awkward marker. This was his stated assumption, based on the first search of the area, that he was dealing with a murder which had taken place elsewhere. The lack of any sign of a struggle was significant but so was the almost complete absence of personal effects to help with identification, such as a handbag and all the usual accoutrements a young woman would generally take with her for an evening out. Tsoutsias was convinced the body had been dumped some time after her death in the field at Vouliagmeni, so he did not expect to encounter items like that. But, before the day was out, a few more crucial articles were discovered, two of which – Ann's driving licence and her address book – gave Tsoutsias a positive identification. These, together with the ring, were found about eight metres from the body. As a senior gendarmerie officer responsible for the Kavouri area, Tsoutsias had of course already seen the missing person report concerning Ann which had been circulated by the Athens suburbs security directorate the previous Saturday. He already suspected that he was dealing with the body of the missing English girl. The discovery of the driving licence and the address book – from which a number of pages had obviously been ripped out – seems to have changed his mood. As soon as he had reported his positive identification of the body, the search was abruptly abandoned; yet customary police practice would suggest an even more thorough scrutiny of the field to see what else might turn up. There can be no doubt that Captain Theodore Tsoutsias was a capable and intelligent officer but he was well aware of the margins of his responsibility in a gendarmerie force operating firmly under the control of a military dictatorship. The decision to allow Ann to be found in the hope that matters would turn out for the best was a catastrophic blunder, because it could not survive even a half-hearted investigation at the scene.

Captain Tsoutsias had made up his mind on his initial

assessment that at least two locations were involved in the crime. Serious problems would emerge if this was allowed to become the dominant theme of the inquiry. Hence, Tsoutsias was instructed to call off the search and order his men back to their nearby post at Vouliagmeni while, in other places, heads were scratched as to what to do next. Clearly, it was essential to supply proof that Ann had indeed been murdered in the field near the bus stop before Tsoutsias and his men returned. A four-day interval ensued, and then came the decision to initiate a second complete sweep of the area, which by now had been furnished with the appropriate evidence. Tsoutsias and his men began again in the early hours of Sunday, 24 October. They were quickly rewarded by the discovery of a pair of light yellow trousers, described as jeans, found tucked under a large boulder which had supposedly been taken from the dry-stone wall at the north of the site. Captain Tsoutsias made no attempt to explain why his men had failed to uncover the trousers during their first search. The trousers were ripped in three places and a few scraps of thorny scrub attached to the seat indicated to Tsoutsias, as he dutifully recorded in his report, that the corpse had been dragged some distance. The evidence as to what Ann was wearing when she left the Pine Hill Hotel has always been conflicting: some witnesses described a short, Indian-style skirt, others a pair of trousers with a zig-zag pattern, and again, darkish or blue jeans. The description which accompanied the missing person alarm distributed on the Saturday evening referred specifically to an Indian-style mini-skirt. Ann's body had been found naked from the waist down, except for a pair of pants, the clear intention being to suggest a sexual motive. The discovery of the trousers, appropriately torn, was intended to support the sex attack theory. Yet, if she had been wearing the jeans and her attacker had torn them off in a frenzy, her legs and thighs would exhibit important signs like cuts and scratches from fingernails. As

112

Kapsaskis had tellingly recorded, these were completely absent. Again, Ann would hardly be likely to submit to such an ordeal without a struggle, and as both Kapsaskis and Tsoutsias saw, the signs of any such struggle were significant by their absence. Indeed, Kapsaskis inadvertently torpedoed the prosecution case right from the start in failing to discover anything – such as scraps of flesh or hair under the fingernails – which might suggest a killing in the course of attempted rape. These obvious contradictions were raised later during Moundis' trial, and the prosecution attempted to side-step them by suggesting that Ann commenced her resistance only when she glimpsed Moundis' wedding ring as they lay together in the field. Edward Chapman has always been outraged by this cruel fantasy.

As if all this were not sufficiently improbable, the events of the following day, Monday 25 October, are totally remarkable. Exactly one week after the discovery of Ann's body, Tsoutsias and his officers were back combing the scene for the third time. This time their search revealed a veritable treasure trove – some thirty-six items altogether, all of them Ann's personal belongings, the entire collection discovered in a very small area near the spot where her body had been found by the snail-collectors. These items all seem to have sprouted like mushrooms overnight. Tsoutsias' embarrassing and inconvenient insistence that Ann had been murdered elsewhere was intended to be undermined by what his men now turned up. Their catalogue of discoveries included sandals, Ann's diary, the programme for the Olympic Holidays visit, an air ticket for the journey to Crete and, of particular significance, a scrap of paper bearing the telephone number of Janet Damen, the BBC's official correspondent in Athens. The condition of Ann's handbag and its contents was in itself most revealing. Scraps of grass inside it indicated a thorough ransacking, the contents having been emptied out and then stuffed back again. Tsoutsias thoughtfully included this conclusion in his report which, by the time he set signature to it on 1 November, had become a textbook of the blunders, confusion and deception which marked the entire eight-day police investigation at Kavouri.

From a careful reading of Tsoutsias' report it is clear that by 25 October, the day of the big finds at Kavouri, Tsoutsias understood that he, like Ann Chapman, was the victim of a conspiracy. He had no alternative but to submit. The grapevine operating inside the investigation services had whispered dangerous hints of political assassination virtually from the moment that Ann's body was discovered. Tsoutsias seems to have selected the only elegant and honourable course to protect his reputation once Greece passed out of the dark years of dictatorship and returned to democracy. He simply committed his own testimony to the official record, illuminated as it is with the revealing passages which make it abundantly clear that Ann was not killed in the field at Kavouri, by a sex maniac or anyone else, but had instead been beaten and strangled at another, then unknown, location. Tsoutsias, and many others like him who knew too many chilling facts, were confident that the restoration of democracy would light the way to justice. What they had not realized was the full extent of the political boundaries which the killing encompassed – boundaries so far-reaching that even the democratic governments which succeeded the Colonels were forced to continue the farce of conspiracy.

The Athens press soon found itself drawn into the plot. The newspapers were fed just enough information about the finding of the body and its subsequent identification to allow coverage of the story as a straightforward police investigation of murder. The government-controlled press agency was given the task of breaking the story and photographs copied from the picture in Ann's passport were also made available to all the principal newspapers in the capital. Greek journalists and correspondents for the international press were all struck by

114

the unusual willingness of the police to talk freely about the case. In fact, they were being drenched with disinformation designed to lead them away from any hint of political intrigue. Even allowing for the fact that the Greek press is not renowned for the quality of its perception, there were obviously severe difficulties in establishing anything like the truth under a military dictatorship. The Athens central police force, which had by now virtually hijacked responsibility for the investigation from the provincial gendarmerie, fed journalists in the capital with a spicy diet of hints about sex as the motive. Not everyone was taken in. A few journalists found subtle ways to signal to their readers individual suspicions about the official line emanating from the police. In the junta-controlled edition of the exiled Helen Vlachos' newspaper, *Kathimerini*, a long report breaking the story of Ann's murder, illustrated with a large photograph, sat uncomfortably alongside the lead item, a lyrical piece about Spiro Agnew and his praise for the regime. On 29 October, *Apogermatini* sailed to the edge of caution by carrying an item which spoke of the 'twelfth day of this mystery, the crime of the past ten years'. The report went on to spotlight the discovery of fingerprints on some of her possessions which had been positively identified as not belonging to Ann. A gendarmerie officer was quoted as believing that they could well belong to the killer. Once again, fact is seen chasing fiction, this time across the inconveniently public columns of the newspapers. After the search of the site at Kavouri, a pretence had been established that torrential rains which fell during the weekend of 15 to 18 October had washed away all traces of fingerprints on Ann's belongings. The story in *Apogermatini* was a provocative contradiction. As control of the investigation slipped to the central police headquarters in Athens, interest in the fingerprints was stifled, so that by the time Moundis came to trial, no forensic evidence of any kind was offered by the prosecution to connect him with Ann.

115

The restrictions under which the Greek press laboured during the junta years can be readily appreciated. Much less explicable is the behaviour of the uncensored BBC – and, in particular, of Ann's employers at Radio London – over the reporting of her death. Radio London's news editors were instructed by official memo not to refer to the girl as either a reporter for the station or a direct employee of the BBC. Technically, the latter was correct, together with the insistence on her freelance status. But Ann's colleagues in the newsroom – especially Mike Brook and Charles Murray – were puzzled by the BBC's insistence at placing distance between the Corporation and the nature of Ann's relationship with it. This policy continued for many years, to the point where news editors and reporters were also actively discouraged from deeper analysis of the ceaseless efforts by Edward Chapman to get at the truth about his daughter's death. The policy of self-imposed censorship by the BBC finally collapsed only when the European Parliament commenced its own inquiry in July 1983. For the first time, journalists at Radio London had the freedom of the air to muse on the fate which had befallen their young colleague who had gone off to Greece in search of a story to make her name.

10 · A Kindness to the Family

If thou shouldst never see my face again,
Pray for my soul.

— Alfred, Lord Tennyson

For Edward and Dorothy Chapman, the long nightmare began in the early hours of Tuesday 19 October. Shortly after 1 a.m., an officer sent from Putney police station woke the couple with the shattering news of Ann's death in Greece. The Chapmans remained in a state of shock for days, consoled by relatives and even at first touchingly comforted by the letter which arrived from the Greek embassy, dated 20 October, which included that fatal time-slip: 'Ever since Sunday, all of us here have followed the news of this reprehensible crime with great concern and anxiety.' Edward Chapman was informed that arrangements were already in hand for the return of his daughter's body by air from the Greek capital. The question of a painful journey to identify her therefore did not arise. The Chapmans did go to Greece but not for another month, on tickets supplied by Basil Mantzos at Olympic Holidays, to discuss the circumstances of Ann's death with the police and gendarmerie officers who had been most involved in the case. In Athens, meanwhile, the question of formal identification had to be settled in accordance with Greek civil law. The Olympic party of travel agents and couriers had continued their official programme, flying on to

Crete before returning directly to London. Any one of them could have been detained or recalled to inspect the corpse at the Athens city mortuary. Instead, this task fell to Basil Mantzos' associate in Greece, Dimitri Lalelis, the host at the brief reception for the Olympic party on the day that Ann disappeared from her hotel. Lalelis remains insistent that he saw Ann only this once, when she joined the other members of the party for drinks in his office. He was a strange choice to perform the identification, being no more than a chance acquaintance. Summoned to the mortuary, he agreed with reasonable confidence that the body he was shown was that of the young woman travelling as a BBC reporter with the Olympic Holidays group. He recalled that her face was badly bruised, evidently from a severe battering and particularly about the right side of the face, around the eye and cheek. Understandably reluctant to linger, Lalelis departed. This was the first of several unusual episodes which surround the identification of Ann's remains, in Greece and London, and the subsequent disposal of the corpse by cremation. In the days which followed Ann's murder, they mark puzzling features of the affair which have never been resolved to Edward Chapman's satisfaction.

Lalelis saw Ann before Dr Kapsaskis began his commendably thorough autopsy. The pre-autopsy photographs taken in the morgue by a photographer from the forensic department reveal much of what Lalelis subsequently described to me. Her features are only just recognizable to a close relative or friend but the severe contusions about the face could pose difficulties for any casual acquaintance. In the course of his work, Kapsaskis took the unusual step of performing a complete facial autopsy. This involved an incision in the flesh along the full extent of the neck to permit complete removal of the facial tissue. The entire procedure was assiduously recorded on film. From this exercise, Kapsaskis was able to deduce the extent of physical damage within the cavity of the head structure. He then loosely re-attached the facial tissue as best he could, before consigning the corpse to an undertaker for embalming. In Greece, this is not a matter of tradition. Then, as now, the city mortuary lacked the facility of refrigeration, and hygiene therefore demands interment within a short time of death. In Ann's case, or in any case involving homicide, the complications would be profound. Decomposition arising from exposure in the field at Kavouri was already well advanced by the time Kapsaskis set to work and naturally accelerated.

The British consul in Athens, Mr E. J. Wise, following normal Foreign Office procedure, accepted responsibility for returning the body of a British citizen to London, and by custom and practice called upon the services of a long-established undertaker in Athens, Nicholas Caloumenos (now dead). He was the agent in Greece for the London-based international undertakers, J. H. Kenyon Ltd, who specialize in the unhappy business of shipping corpses about the globe. Caloumenos worked quickly and Ann's remains were air-freighted to London on 25 October, the account for 39,000 drachmas being posted off to J. H. Kenyon the following day. The details of the account tendered by Nicholas Caloumenos are important because of the controversy which arose over the identification of Ann's body at Kenyon's premises in London. The charges included placing the corpse inside a special air-tight container, which was then hermetically sealed at the main Athens cemetery in the presence of customs, health and currency authorities, all of whom were present to fulfil their own particular bureaucratic rites. For shipment to London, the air-tight container was placed inside a cheap, plain beechwood coffin, and then finally within an anonymous air-freight crate. Kenyon's handle hundreds of consignments like this every year and in many cases, like that of Ann, they contain the victims of tragedy and misfortune. In order to open the sealed container specialist attention is required, and Kenyon's, like all their competitors, make a point of charging for it. On this occasion they did not do so.

The Greek undertaker Caloumenos, still remembered in Athens today as a sensitive master of his craft, was sufficiently worried by what he had seen of Ann to send a private note to Kenyon's via the British consul, Mr Wise. He suggested it would be a kindness to spare her family the sight of her remains. What happened to this message is not clear but, in the event, neither of the Chapmans ever saw Ann. Some years later, Edward Chapman sought further clarification from Caloumenos who confirmed in a letter that the body certainly was 'in such a condition as to cause a terrible shock to the relatives'. This clear, unambiguous assessment from the man who received Ann's body from the mortuary and then prepared it for despatch to London is hard to square with subsequent accounts of the condition of the corpse.

Ann's body was flown to London in the cargo hold of a BEA jet. Kenyon's had a hearse ready at the airport to transfer it to their main reception rooms in London, while arrangements for the funeral were made by the family. Still numbed by shock, Edward and Dorothy Chapman could not bring themselves to identify Ann. Dorothy's brother at first volunteered, but in the meantime the Rev. Blennerhassett, the station padre at Radio London, visited the family to offer spiritual comfort and while there agreed to take the task upon himself. In 1983 I went to see Rev. Blennerhassett in his home in the Portsmouth suburb of Southsea and he then recalled: 'When I was with Mr and Mrs Chapman they brought up the matter of having the body identified and seemed very reluctant to do it. I wanted to do what I could to relieve the tension. I asked whether they would like me to do it.' Edward Chapman later thought that the offer for the Rev. Blennerhassett to intercede came first from the station manager at Radio London, Peter Redhouse. Blennerhassett remembered discussing the proposition with Redhouse and then with

Kenyon's. 'I explained who I was and asked if I could come to identify the body. They said that they closed at five or half past but there was a door at the side still open and I arranged to go at six, or it may have been later, half past six or seven.'

Rev. Blennerhassett declares that he went along as arranged and, after ringing the bell at the side door, was met by a man in a white coat. 'I went upstairs. The coffin was in the middle of the room with the lid off. The body was dressed in a shroud. It just looked like Ann.' He saw nothing which could possibly account for the note of caution sent to Kenyon's by the undertaker Nicholas Caloumenos. Blennerhassett was firm in his memory of relatively tranquil, composed features inside the coffin which had arrived from Athens. Describing Ann's appearance he told me: 'Yellowish did not mean the ivory kind I associate with the faces of dead people: brownish might have been more accurate and my wife remembers me saying, "It was going brown around the edges." What happens to a banana when it is going off was, I think, what I intended by the word "going" . . .'

Two years after Ann's death, Edward Chapman began to investigate the possibility that the hermetically sealed casket and beechwood coffin which arrived from Athens had not after all contained the body of his daughter. He wrote to J. H. Kenyon and was stunned to receive the following reply from one of their senior managers, Mr P. J. Harris. First, the question of a death certificate: 'An autopsy report was not produced and we saw no certificate giving details of cause of death.' The letter, of 25 October 1973, then raised severe problems over the identification of Ann's remains by the Rev. Eric Blennerhassett. 'The zinc casket that your daughter was in was not opened and the hermetical seal was not broken. No person in this country saw her and it is therefore impossible to give details of any external injuries.' Rev. Blennerhassett was immediately approached by Edward Chapman but still remained insistent that he had identified Ann, despite the assertion by Kenyon's that 'no person in this country saw her'. A year later, Mr Harris wrote to Mr Chapman again from the company's office in Edgware Road, amplifying in detail the reasons why Ann's corpse had never been inspected by anyone in London:

> I have questioned all the staff members concerning the possibility of anyone viewing the remains after the arrival in London. No one recalls such an event and our records indicate that the metallic seal on the inner coffin was not broken. Additionally, no preservative treatment was given and no part of the original casket replaced, as would probably have been required had the casket been opened. Further, no charge was made in the account for opening the casket, as should have been made had this work been carried out.

By April 1974 relations between Edward Chapman and Rev. Blennerhassett were frosty, as is revealed in a letter from the clergyman: 'I was personally confident that the face which I looked at was the face of your daughter, Ann.' Kenyon's were also disturbed by the potential embarrassment which could ensue from a dispute with a clergyman, and Blennerhassett's letter includes this sentence:

> A Mr Kenyon to whom I spoke at their head office points out that their letter did make clear that these were the facts according to their records, but he agrees that if he had written the letter – and especially if he had known that I was stating otherwise, he would have worded it very differently. He says that nobody at Kenyons now, or at the time of writing that letter, remembers one way or another.

Yet both letters from Mr Harris were commendably thorough and precise, indicating the lengths to which he went – questioning staff, inspecting the records and accounts – in order to satisfy Edward Chapman.

In my long interview with the Rev. Blennerhassett at Southsea, he remained positive that Ann's corpse had lain only in a plain, traditional-style coffin, with no sign of the second, inner casket in which her body had been despatched from Athens. Her features apparently revealed nothing of the severe battering she had received, the effects of subsequent decomposition from exposure in the field at Kavouri, or the extensive and further disfiguring facial autopsy performed by Professor Kapsaskis. Edward Chapman was not alone in his doubts. Professor David Bowen, head of the forensic department at Charing Cross Hospital medical school, whom Chapman had consulted on so many aspects concerning his daughter's death, told me in July 1983: 'If the body arrived in the UK on the 25th October, a lapse of ten days after death, it would be quite decomposed and it would be hard for close relatives to identify her. Embalming would improve the situation but it would still be difficult.'

In his discussion with me, the Rev. Blennerhassett recalled Ann's features only as going 'brownish' at the edges. Yet in correspondence with Edward Chapman's solicitor, Geoffrey Bindman, in October 1982, Blennerhassett suggested that he was not always so certain about that description. He told Bindman, that he could not say 'anything' about the condition of the body. During the course of the European Parliament inquiry, I talked to Kenyon's again. Time, they said, had now erased all record of the event and the conflicting claims which had been made. But Mr Harris, who is now a senior director of the company and travels the world helping relatives to identify the victims of every conceivable kind of tragedy, did agree that, had he known at the time of his correspondence with Edward Chapman that Kapsaskis had performed a facial autopsy, he might have proposed that that in itself would make the task of practical identification exceedingly difficult.

123

The fact is that no one can ever be certain that Ann actually was in that coffin which was sent to London from Athens. Later, the authorities were at pains to suggest to the Chapman family that everything had been done by the letter of the law, although the law would be later considered wholly inadequate to meet the circumstances which arise from the violent death of British citizens abroad. Ann's remains were duly cremated at Putney Vale crematorium, the Rev. Blennerhassett conducting the service.

The medical officer of health for the area later told Edward Chapman that cremation had taken place without the formalities of an inquest in Britain, or presentation of a death certificate, on the basis of an order from the Home Secretary, at that time the late Reginald Maudling, stating that neither was required. The legal basis of that interpretation lay in the arcane depths of the Coroners Act, 1887, and, in particular, in the meaning of the word 'jurisdiction'. Section one of the Act declares that a coroner is obliged to conduct an inquest whenever he is informed that a dead body lies within his jurisdiction and there is 'reasonable cause' to suspect that such a person has met a violent or unnatural death. The late Mr Gavin Thurston, the coroner for West London, within whose jurisdiction Ann most definitely if temporarily lay, did not hold such an inquest and nor did the Home Office propose that action as a precaution against any irregularities which might have occurred in Greece. Mr Thurston wrote to Edward Chapman: 'It is unlikely that any inquiry in England would have served a useful purpose – it would have been impossible to summon witnesses from abroad and information would necessarily have been documentary or hearsay.' Yet many of the crucial witnesses had returned to England well before Ann's remains, on the jet which flew the party of Olympic travel agents directly back from Crete. They included one of the last people to see Ann alive, Nicholas Clarkson.

Professor David Bowen of Charing Cross Hospital thought it 'fraught with danger' that no post-mortem, let alone an inquest, had taken place in London. Edward Chapman is convinced that the British authorities connived at the minimum of formalities in Britain to avoid raising awkward questions over Ann's fate. It is possible that someone in Greece indulged in body substitution, some time after the post-mortem was completed, and before Ann's supposed remains were despatched to London. This would account for the dramatic difference between what the Rev. Eric Blennerhassett described after his visit to Kenyon's and the appalling state of the corpse revealed in the official photographs taken at the morgue. But the substitution argument still does not settle the contradiction arising from Kenyon's conviction that Ann, or whoever it was in the coffin, had never been identified in any case. Certainly, once the remains had been consigned to the incinerator at Putney Vale crematorium, these questions lay beyond answer.

Years later, the tragic death of another young British girl abroad would lead to the wholesale review of the operation of the 1887 Coroners Act. The only distinctly significant difference separating the case of Ann and that of Helen Smith, a British nurse working in Saudi Arabia who fell, or was pushed, from the balcony of a block of flats in Jeddah, lay in the fact that Helen's body remained in Britain preserved by refrigeration. But the Court of Appeal did not base its judgement on that fact alone. In what became a *cause célèbre*, Helen's father, Mr Ronald Smith, fought a prolonged legal battle to force the West Yorkshire coroner to hold an inquest. His victory came when the Court of Appeal sat in July 1982. Two of the three judges, sitting under Lord Lane, the Lord Chief Justice, concluded that the cornerstone of the 1887 Act was the phrase 'jurisdiction'. Their Lordships' majority verdict stated that a coroner had 'no discretion' in interpretation of the Act and that 'territoriality was provided by the presence of the body within the area for which the coroner had responsibility'. Edward and Dorothy Chapman read the judgement with a good deal of bitterness. It proved conclusively that Gavin Thurston had been wrong to insist that he had no right to call an inquest and summon witnesses, simply because Ann had met her death in Greece. For a short period, between the arrival of the remains at Heathrow and their subsequent cremation in Putney Vale, the corpse was within his territorial jurisdiction. The fact that Ann had met a violent death was perfectly well known to the Foreign Office, which handled the arrangements for the return to Britain, and in turn to the Home Office, whose political master, Reginald Maudling, had permitted cremation without the precaution of post-mortem or inquest in Britain.

The Chapmans now judge these events as evidence of suspicious and unseemly haste by the British authorities. Ann's death in Greece was already the source of major embarrassment to the British intelligence community, and to the British government, who wished to make as little of the affair as possible. Gavin Thurston probably would have held an inquest had he been prompted to do so by the Home Office. But this action would have trailed even bigger stories across the front page of every newspaper in Britain and beyond, seriously compromising the official line coming out of Greece that Ann was the unfortunate and chance victim of a brutal sex attacker. Ann's body would then require positive and thorough identification, and not just a kindly offer to spare the family's grief from a clergyman who had known Ann only casually during her months at Radio London. A fresh post-mortem would reveal the extent of the work already done by Dr Kapsaskis in Athens, and the terrible injuries to Ann's face. The Chapmans might well suspect a good deal more than a sexual attack had they themselves viewed their daughter's remains. This path looked treacherous and dictated the shortest possible route to a crematorium — in the event, precisely the one that Ann's remains took. Those who charted this course could not have reckoned on the tenacity with which Ann's father would pursue the truth behind the long, muddled conspiracy.

126

11 · Tickets for the Odyssey

All professions are conspiracies against the laity

— George Bernard Shaw

Three weeks after Ann's cremation at Putney, Edward and Dorothy Chapman flew to Greece using tickets supplied by Olympic Holidays. This was the first of more than a dozen visits over the years on which the couple spent their life savings in search of the truth. What little news they received via the British consul in Athens suggested that the Greek authorities had not progressed very far in the search for Ann's killer. The Chapmans arrived in the Greek capital determined to find out what exactly was being done by the police. Edward Chapman knew enough of the condition of the country to suspect some kind of political implication. Ann's last words to her parents, her mission to secure 'the big story', still rang in their ears.

From the moment they arrived in Greece, the Chapmans were treated to the elaborate pretence that the police and gendarmerie were sparing no effort to track down the person or persons responsible for a brutal, criminal act. Edward Chapman's suspicions of conspiracy were deftly side-tracked, in a most convincing manner, by the gendarmerie officer placed in overall command of the inquiry, Colonel Papantri-anfyllou. He had a three-hour meeting with Edward Chapman, skilfully crafted to allay fears that the Greek government

127

or its agents were involved in Ann's death. 'I came away completely brainwashed,' Edward Chapman recalled later. 'I had at first thought that Ann's death was political but they convinced me otherwise.' Papantrianfyllou did his job well, but still managed to transmit something else during the encounter which Edward Chapman sensed as 'a remarkable degree of compassion for a police investigator', the intuitive feeling that had Papantrianfyllou been free, he might have told Chapman a good deal more. Later, Chapman began writing to Papantrianfyllou, bombarding him with letters sent through the diplomatic bag to the British embassy in Athens. The authorities there eventually tired of being used as a post office, but for a while Papantrianfyllou's sympathetic and considered responses to Chapman's detailed questions were received regularly in Putney. And then the link was abruptly snapped. In April 1972 the replies stopped coming. Edward Chapman was bluntly informed that Papantrianfyllou had been 'transferred to other duties' – in other words, he was beyond the reach of the increasingly sensitive probes directed by the father of the dead woman. Papantrianfyllou was replaced by Major, later Colonel, Goundras who had been involved in the case from the beginning. When the British consul, Mr Wise, sent news of this to the Chapmans he included an assessment of how police inquiries were proceeding and gave an account of a meeting with Goundras whom he graphically described as peering over a massive three-volume file containing well over 600 pages. 'I sleep with this file,' Goundras declared. Mr Wise told the Chapmans that the police were asking anyone arrested for sexual crimes to account for their movements on the night of 15–16 October 1971: 'The police are still of the opinion that the motive for the murder which they gave you last November is the real one.'

Despite the strongest pressure from Edward Chapman, the British police refused to mount any separate investigation in Britain or to send officers to Greece to assist the local investigations into the death of a British citizen. Scotland Yard never became involved except to act as agents for any inquiries the Greeks required to be made in London. Chapman nevertheless went to Scotland Yard on many occasions and was disturbed to see that the meagre operation there was in the hands of a junior officer. After one particularly vigorous encounter demanding more action, he was told sharply: 'You don't want an international incident, do you?'

In 1974, Robert (later Lord) Carr, who was then the Chapmans' Conservative MP in Putney, raised the issue in the Commons. The Foreign Secretary, James Callaghan, supplied an answer which over the years has stuck like a needle caught in the groove of a record: 'So far as the Foreign and Commonwealth Office are concerned, it is the responsibility of the local authorities to make whatever inquiries are necessary when a United Kingdom citizen dies abroad.' When Callaghan gave that answer, Moundis was already in gaol for the manslaughter of Ann, a verdict which Chapman and his legal advisers had rejected.

Edward Chapman's insistence on a political motive behind his daughter's death failed to evince the slightest reaction from the British authorities, who consistently backed first the Greek police and then the Greek courts, despite the fact that the British embassy in Athens knew full well that both were under the political influence of the military junta. The correspondence which began shortly after Ann's death between Edward Chapman, the embassy and consular officials in Athens and then the Foreign Office in London, supplies an intriguing picture of the lengths to which the British authorities went in their extraordinary compromise with the Greek regime over Ann's death. Edward Chapman was given the diplomatic brush-off, at first in the politest possible terms, right from the beginning. In December 1972, well before the trial of Moundis, he was wrestling to understand the meaning of his rights in Greek as a '*partie civile*'. This was the advice from the Foreign Office: 'If you are in any doubt about this, I can only suggest that you yourself should seek from the Greek embassy in London an authoritative explanation of your position under Greek law.' This was an indication of how little assistance British representatives in Greece were prepared to provide for one of their own puzzled and confused citizens trying to get to grips with the tragedy of a daughter murdered in a foreign country. In February 1973, this nugget of correspondence was received by Edward Chapman, above the signature of the same official:

> I well understand and can sympathize with your intention to examine all the evidence you can in your efforts to arrive at the truth about your daughter's death. You may feel that our response to your inquiries has sometimes been rather negative. This has not meant that we lack sympathy to help a British subject but simply reflects certain constraints that we have no choice but to respect.

No elaboration was ever offered to explain the precise definition of those 'constraints'. The row kicked up by Edward Chapman, his noisy allegations of a political conspiracy and a cover-up involving complicity between the Greek and British governments, was already assuming more than purely nuisance value to the British authorities. It had become a thorough political embarrassment. In April 1973, Hugh Jenkins, the former Labour MP for Putney, tried to press the British government to nominate a senior Foreign Office official to re-examine the case on the basis of Chapman's continuing allegations. Jenkins was sharply turned down by Anthony Kershaw, Parliamentary Under-Secretary at the Foreign Office, in one of the exchanges in the Commons over Ann's death. A month later, the Foreign Office tried to signal to Chapman that their patience had run out and he should

130

drop the affair. He was instructed by the Foreign Office to cease pestering their officials in Greece and London with questions. 'Whilst we sincerely sympathize with you and Mrs Chapman over the death of your daughter, we cannot continue to undertake what are essentially private inquiries.' Chapman still refused to give up. By August the British consul in Athens, Mr Wise, was refusing to respond to his letters, pleading pressure of work and lack time for embassy staff to handle so many detailed inquiries. In any case, argued Wise, 'I do not believe that any other force could have pursued their investigation more thoroughly than the Greeks.' Chapman's letters were in future intercepted by the consular department at Petty France in London. He was told tetchily by an official there: 'I cannot accept your claim that anything about the case is being covered up.' It would, of course, be too much to expect a frank admission from the Foreign Office that the police investigations into Ann's death had been rigged, along with the trial of Nicholas Moundis, but the stumbling efforts of the British authorities to maintain the pretence that justice had been done look absurd when submitted to the judgement of passing years.

Everyone in Greece, including the eyes and ears of the British government inside the Athens embassy, knew that Kapsaskis would obligingly dance to any tune called by the junta. By 'adapting' forensic evidence, he had been thoroughly implicated in a scandal which had rocked the country in the early sixties, the so-called affair of 'Z', in which a communist MP was brutally tortured and murdered by the secret police. Throughout the tenure of the Colonels' regime, he obligingly contorted and twisted the truth to enable the courts to serve up false judgements. Yet Chapman was told by the Foreign Office, when he started to question the discrepancies between the first post-mortem on Ann's body conducted by Kapsaskis and later contradictions at the trial of Moundis: 'As regards the autopsy report, there was no reason for the Consul to press the Greek authorities for this, since there was no reason to suppose that

131

they were neglecting their duties.' In truth, the officials inside Edward Chapman's own embassy in Athens had *every* reason to suspect the manner in which the Greek authorities had gone about their inquiries into Ann's death from the moment the body was found. The persistent refusal to co-operate with Edward Chapman and supply answers to vital questions was a deliberate policy of non co-operation.

The embassy insisted it had no record of the date on which Ann's passport had been handed in – yet officials had also told Chapman that the passport had been in Dr Kapsaskis' possession when he began the autopsy. The date on which the embassy received the passport is crucial because it illustrates the extent to which the authorities had been preparing their cover-up after Ann was murdered on the night of 15–16 October. If the passport was already in the hands of Kapsaskis when he set to work early on the morning of 19 October, it suggests a remarkable dexterity by the authorities in tracing Ann's identity and, more significantly, getting hold of the document, either from her room at the Pine Hill Hotel, or subtracting it from her belongings later found scattered around the field at Kavouri. Neither could the embassy supply a practical explanation as to why a copy of the autopsy report was not forwarded to London, except to insist, as officialdom always can, that it was 'not normal practice'.

As the years progressed and Chapman's determination did not fade, it was remarkable how the Foreign Office revealed the paucity of its duties in the case of a British citizen who met a violent death abroad. In 1974 it was admitted, for example, that 'the embassy in Athens did not check the documents that accompanied the coffin to London', a strange neglect of elementary precautions in a case of murder. The embassy was trustingly prepared to leave all responsibility for identification of the body and accuracy of any documentation concerned with it entirely to the local authorities – this at a time when an illegal military government had been branded before world opinion as a cruel and vindictive persecutor of its own citizens.

Edward Chapman was desperately keen to establish contact with Brian Rawson – who had reported Ann missing to the British embassy – and with the Olympic courier, Lynda Nichol. He eventually succeeded in talking to Lynda Nichol but never to Brian Rawson. By 1974, when Chapman was harrying the Foreign Office vigorously for help on these and other questions, a conviction that Ann had been the victim of a political plot was becoming widespread in both Britain and Greece. But even after the collapse of the junta in the wake of the Cyprus invasion, the Foreign Office and, through it, successive British governments, refused to budge an inch from the official line that justice had been done. In Putney, meanwhile, Hugh Jenkins MP continued to pester the Foreign Office with political salvos on Chapman's behalf. In August 1975 Roy Hattersley, who had become Minister of State at the Foreign Office under the incoming Labour government, sent a long letter to Jenkins, brusquely rejecting Edward Chapman's contention that embassy and consular officials had been less than helpful. Hattersley said that no one in the Foreign Office had found any evidence to back up Chapman's allegations of conspiracy in three and a half years of dealing with the case. Both Edward and Dorothy Chapman had been insisting that they had never received the message, passed fom the undertaker Caloumenos to the consul, and then to Kenyon's in London, that Ann's body would represent a distressing sight to her parents. Edward Chapman insists that had he known of this message he would never have given permission for Ann to be buried, let alone cremated. Roy Hattersley declared there was 'nothing sinister' about the nature of the message, or the manner of its passing to Kenyon's, but even allowing for the Chapmans' distress at the time, it is clear that had the disturbing suggestion of Ann's body being 'an unpleasant sight' reached them, they would have reacted differently. The consul was later to say that he 'bitterly regretted' his action in passing on the message from the undertakers, because of what he thought the Chapmans had made of it. Interwoven with the confusing affair of the identification of Ann by the Rev. Eric Blennerhassett, it is not surprising that the Chapmans came to doubt that Ann was actually in the coffin flown back to London. If British officials in Athens had established a positive identity and not, in their own words, simply left it to the 'competent local authorities', then the Foreign Office might have been spared many of Chapman's accusations of complicity. Hattersley's letter to Hugh Jenkins concluded with this advice to Edward Chapman: 'It would be wrong of me to leave him with the impression that there is anything more that we can do to help him.' The Foreign Office had evidently concluded that the matter was closed and that Edward Chapman's attempts to fight his way to the truth would fail. They were wrong.

In the spring of 1976, the diplomatic bag returning from Athens to London contained news of the sensational development that the Greeks were, after all, preparing to give Moundis another opportunity to prove his innocence. Chapman's only way of tracing Ann's real killers was to get Moundis out of prison and pardoned. This, his lawyers believed, would force the Greeks back to square one. In the event, the attempt would fail, but the re-hearing staged by the Greek appeal court was in fact a considerable triumph for Chapman and Moundis' own lawyer, John Theodoru – a man with the reputation of being one of the most formidable advocates in criminal law in Greece. The stout line of defence adopted by the Foreign Office over the years began to look decidedly shaky. Chapman, on hearing news of the re-trial, at once wrote to the British authorities again repeating his plea for help; but the official line remained firm. A British citizen who had been virtually abandoned by his own government in the search for justice was told it would not be

LEFT: Theodoru (arm raised), still one of the most formidable criminal lawyers in Greece, makes an impassioned plea for the innocence of his client, who watches anxiously from the dock (top left).

BELOW: But the guilt of Moundis had been assured before the court even sat. Moundis is handcuffed at the start of his life-term. He left the court shouting his innocence.

LEFT: America's 'clerical Castro', Archbishop Makarios (left), president of independent Cyprus, tried hard to keep in step with the Greek junta led by Col. George Papadopoulos (right). Yet later he would speak of a premonition that a hand was reaching out from Athens 'to terminate my earthly existence'. It almost did.

BELOW: Turkish troops triumphant on Cypriot soil. The date is 20 July 1974. Within days the Greek junta will collapse and Cyprus will be politically divided – the final solution.

RIGHT: The man of the people. The Greek socialist premier Andreas Papandreou casts his vote in the 1985 general election which won him a second term of office. Papandreou is by now pursuing highly antagonistic policies towards Turkey and the USA.

BELOW: Brothers in harmony – for the time being. Constantine Karamanlis (left), first premier of Greece after the collapse of the junta, greets his Turkish opposite number, Suleiman Demirel. The two men tried hard to submerge the Cyprus issue. Karamanlis was to be ousted in a constitutional coup, Demirel banned from politics by the Turkish army.

ABOVE: The mystery in the Thames. Kotsias, senior Olympic Holidays courier during Ann's trip to Greece, drowned trying to rescue a woman when his car dived out of a pub car-park into the flooding river.

RIGHT: Nearing the end of the trail. The author (right) with Edward Chapman (left) and Ann's mother, Dorothy (foreground), in the offices of John Theodoru (centre), the remarkable Athens lawyer who never relented in his own quest to prove the innocence of Moundis.

'appropriate or advisable' for Her Majesty's government to make any further intervention with the Greek authorities, lest such action be interpreted as an 'unwarranted interference in their legal process'. So Chapman was still virtually alone apart from Theodoru.

The following year, in September 1977, Chapman received the only letter that came to him unprompted from the Foreign Office – a bill for £542.43 for flying Ann's remains back to London, with the threat of legal proceedings unless he paid up promptly. The Chapmans had been refusing to pay the bill to maintain at least a residual grip on the Foreign Office over their role in dealing with Ann's body. So in turn the Foreign Office received a stubborn reply from Chapman. As a man who had received 100 drachmas (about £1) from the Greek authorities in compensation for the grief he and his wife had suffered over the death of their daughter, he would not consider 'your application for payment' until the truth had been found. In November the Foreign Office called a halt to Chapman's attempts to use the diplomatic bag travelling to Athens to send messages to his own Greek lawyer, Lykourezos. 'I am so sorry that we cannot use our channels of communication in this way,' Chapman was told. He was asked to collect his package and inquire if the Greek embassy in London would handle it instead.

In December, Labour's new Foreign Secretary, David Owen, was asked to respond to Chapman's logic: since the former dictators were now themselves in prison for deceiving the Greek people, would the British government at last intervene, after six years of prevarication? Owen himself did not reply but an official from the consular department did. The needle remained firmly stuck in the groove: 'I am afraid that I have to tell you that the British embassy in Athens will be unable to support your proposed approach to the Greek authorities.'

Hugh Jenkins was still doggedly persisting in his attempts

to prise open the firmly closed door to the Foreign Office. In August 1978 he tried again to get the Foreign Office to propose what, if any, legal action might be attempted to assist a British citizen seeking justice. The reply he received contained the remarkable assertion that Chapman himself seemed to be to blame, because he had not pursued the opportunity of acquiring '*partie civile*' status at the original trial of Moundis. Yet when Chapman had sought advice over his anxieties on that very point, he had been rebuffed by the Foreign Office. They would even claim, wrongly, that Chapman had voluntarily abandoned his *partie civile* status in the case of Moundis, whereas he had merely chosen not to exercise his rights – rights which were well enough understood when they were explained to Hugh Jenkins in September 1978, but not apparently at the time when Edward Chapman desperately required help from his own embassy in understanding his legal position.

As the years rolled by, socialists and conservatives enjoying their respective tenures at the Foreign Office all refused to help the Chapmans. The Conservative minister, Ian Gilmour, wrote to them at the end of 1979: 'Hard though I appreciate it must be for you to accept, I am afraid that there is really nothing more the government can do to help you.' An ambitious young Tory politician, David Mellor, who succeeded Hugh Jenkins in the Putney seat, took up the cudgels for Chapman and even managed to win an adjournment debate on Ann, using the opportunity of the Commons discussion on Greek accession to the European Community. Mellor – who would, ironically, eventually find himself a minister in the Home Office – had the same wearily depressing replies. That from Lord Belstead to Mellor in May 1983 maintained the tone: 'I am sorry that we cannot do more to help Mr Chapman but I really think we have done all we can.' As soon as I was appointed by the European Parliament to mount a new investigation, the Foreign Office informed Edward

Chapman that they would 'give whatever help we properly can' both in London and at the Athens embassy. In the event, I enjoyed a short and quite unrevealing interview with the ambassador, at that time Sir Peregrine Rhodes, who regretted very much that he and his officials could offer very little of substantial value 'beyond what is already known'.

Late in 1986, Edward Chapman intercepted rumours of another re-trial of Moundis. The consular department at the Foreign Office wrote to me: 'In respect to your suggestion that an Embassy representative should attend such a hearing, we do not think this would be necessary. The hearing would be in public, and would very probably be reported fully in the press.' In fact, reports of a fresh initiative by Theodoru on behalf of Moundis proved still-born.

In 1971, even before the machinery of the Greek state was set in motion against an innocent man, the police continued to pump the embassy and consulate in Athens with stories which supported the sexual motive. No one in the service of the British government saw fit to challenge an assumption which flew in the face of 'the facts'. Yet the conclusion of Captain Tsoutsias, the first officer to arrive on the scene at Kavouri, subsequently supported by the post-mortem conducted by Kapsaskis, that Ann had not been sexually abused was well known to everyone at the embassy. When the apparently sympathetic Papantrianfyllou was replaced by Goundras in April 1972, the Chapmans decided to call the Greeks' bluff. In August Dorothy Chapman wrote a deliberately provocative letter to the Greek authorities via the British ambassador. She made the accusation: 'The police must be hiding something,' adding that she and her husband knew the identity of Ann's killer. The effect of this bombshell was astonishing. Within days of the letter arriving in Athens, it was announced that a former prison guard had been arrested and charged with the attempted rape and murder of Ann Dorothy Chapman.

12 · A Perfect Victim

He vexed time, and busied the whole state
Troubled both foes and friends, but ever to no ends!

—Ben Jonson

The choice of Nicholas Moundis as scapegoat for the murder
of Ann Chapman appeared at first to be a stroke of genius.
His credentials as a sexual voyeur, including one previous
conviction for a serious offence against a young woman and
his habit of frequenting the woods around Kavouri to spy on
courting couples, were perfect. Moundis was also at a great
disadvantage because of his presence in Kavouri on the day
that Ann was killed and because he had not denied he could
have been near the Pine Hill Hotel at about the time that she
walked out, allegedly heading for the bus stop and the bus to
downtown Athens. Moundis was such an ideal suspect that
he was in fact picked up at a very early stage in the inquiry
and questioned by gendarmerie officers working, they insisted, from a list of well-known sexual offenders. But
Moundis was then able to produce and sustain a watertight
alibi: he had been nowhere near Kavouri at the material time,
when the forensic report revealed that Ann had actually been
strangled, at around midnight on 15 October, and could
produce his father-in-law, the taxi driver, as proof.

Moundis was an unattractive character, thick-set, indifferent to work or domestic routine and possessed of a passing

regard for the truth. He was preoccupied with the search for extra-marital sex on any occasion he could escape from the house, even if he was restricted to prowling round his favourite resort, Kavouri, and getting thrills from watching courting couples. His wife knew all about her husband's grubby extra-curricular activities but his father-in-law who detested him never once wavered in his insistence that he had picked up Moundis and taken him home at the time when all the evidence proves that Ann was still alive. This crushing blow to the prosecution's case was ignored at the trial and at every subsequent trawl through the affair. Much more was made of Moundis as a man with an unpleasant and malicious reputation who would easily kill in the course of a frustrated sexual encounter.

From 1958 until 1968, Moundis had actually been in the employ of the state, as a prison guard – a job which offered reasonably good pay by Greek standards and even conferred on him a kind of status. Moundis threw it all away in 1968 when he lost control and attacked a seventeen-year-old girl on his home island of Aegina. The record of this event has, like so much else in the Chapman affair, been seriously distorted in many accounts. Moundis did not attempt murder or rape but his attack so frightened the girl that she fainted. He masturbated over her prostrate body and then stole the transistor radio she was carrying. For this offence he went before a military court, because of his job in the prison service, and was given a four-year sentence for assault. After two years he was freed on parole, during which period he was compelled to report regularly to the police. The station selected for these appointments was in the Athens maritime suburb of Piraeus, whose territorial responsibility included Aegina, about an hour away by boat or thirty minutes in today's high-speed 'Flying Dolphin' jetfoils. By another of those ironic twists of circumstance, among the senior officers whom Moundis saw regularly at Piraeus was Yannis Yannoulis, who later arrested him on the charge of murdering Ann Chapman. When the time came for

139

Moundis to be rounded up and accused of killing Ann, the propositions made by Yannoulis were not ones he felt he could easily resist. But in his own clumsy fashion, Moundis foisted a personal act of revenge on Yannoulis by trying to implicate him in the plot to kill Ann. This deliberate act of confusion by Moundis, understandable though it is as revenge for twelve years spent behind bars, has thrown many investigators off the track of those who really did kill Ann. The real significance of Yannoulis' role lies in the manner in which Moundis was selected as the chosen candidate to bear responsibility for Ann's death, thus solving a mysterious crime and at the same time silencing the dangerous claims of a top-level political conspiracy.

Nicholas Moundis, unconsciously, took the first steps towards many years in prison several days before Ann arrived in Athens. On 12 October, a Tuesday, he started a regular period of eight days' leave from the small factory where he worked. On the 14th, the day before Ann died, his brother-in-law had a serious accident at work and was taken to the city's main King Paul Hospital. At around five o'clock on the 14th, Moundis went with a friend to visit his brother-in-law, but in the event he stayed outside the hospital to 'guard' the car, a brand-new taxi. In his customary fashion, Moundis started chatting and showing off to a girl who caught his eye while he smoked and gossiped in the porter's lodge outside the hospital. He spotted an attractive opportunity for an interesting diversion during his week's break from the factory and arranged to meet the girl the following day, Friday the 15th, at his favourite hunting-ground at Kavouri. Moundis would say later that he was furious when the girl did not turn up to keep the rendezvous, and decided to expend some of his frustrations by pottering off around the woods looking for couples to watch. He claimed that during this perambulation of the area he failed to find any courting couples, but encountered instead a very odd group of people lurking in the bushes near the Pine Hill Hotel. These included no lesser figures than Yannis Yannoulis and the brother of the dictator, Charalambos Papadopoulos, who was charged with responsibility for state security. This was the lie Moundis later concocted to place the blame for Ann's death where he thought it lay.

But there is another, more compelling version of events in Kavouri that day, which would suggest that Moundis had been telling part of the truth about a rendezvous with a girl and which accounts for the claim, later made in court, that Moundis had been scratched and had blood on his shirt when he arrived home. This can be deduced from a careful analysis of the statements taken by the police from almost everyone in the area of the Pine Hill Hotel who had anything significant to say about unusual events on 15 October. One contributor was called Balaskas, a petrol attendant working at the filling station near the Kavouri crossroads. He said in a sworn deposition to Major Goundras that at around 6.30 on the evening of the 15th, a young woman asked if she could use the telephone. He directed her to the nearby Bana roadside café, where Balaskas later went himself and chatted over a coffee to a friend, Theodore Oeconomides, who worked there as a waiter. The subject of a young woman soon came up and Oeconomides had interesting gossip to relate. The girl who came to the café was in a distressed state, 'crying and was begging for me to phone for a taxi'. More than that, she complained about being attacked by 'a cousin'. She admitted she had been out with him twice before, but this time he flung himself at her and ripped her stockings in a mad passion. Oeconomides also made his own statement to Major Goundras. The girl told him she had arranged to meet her cousin in a local taverna but when they left he suddenly leapt on her 'with the intention of rape'. A taxi took about fifteen minutes to come from nearby Vouliagmeni and as soon as it arrived the distressed young woman departed. Afterwards, both Balaskas and Oeconomides recalled seeing a stranger,

141

between thirty and thirty-five they thought, hanging around the area. He was stocky, athletically built, with brown hair beginning to thin, a description bearing more than a passing resemblance to the way Moundis looked in 1971. John Talbot, it will be remembered, had also seen a similar figure exercising energetically on the beach near the Pine Hill Hotel, while Ann was sunbathing not far away. The man observed by Balaskas and Oeconomides hovered around the Kavouri crossroads, near the St Nicholas bus stop, and then walked off. Balaskas remembered, crucially, that there were several people at the bus stop, waiting for the bus to Athens. 'From that moment I lost him, being preoccupied in my business.'

Oeconomides made his first statement to Goundras on 21 October, when it had already been decided to present Ann's murder as an act of sexual violence. Three days later, Oeconomides went to see Goundras again and on this occasion insisted that he knew the young woman who had appeared in his café complaining of attempted rape. He added, in a telling phrase: 'Besides, she herself recognized me.' Oeconomides clearly believed, in volunteering this second statement, that he was offering the gendarmerie vital information. Goundras, who had succeeded Theodore Tsoutsias as the senior gendarmerie officer investigating the crime, never denied that he was looking for a sexually-orientated criminal, but he chose to ignore what the waiter had to say. Here, within days of Ann's death, the gendarmerie had a clear link with a man who was in the area at the material time, and who could readily and easily be identified as a potential killer of Ann Chapman. The waiter Oeconomides knew the name of the young woman who had alleged attempted rape, not by a total stranger, but by her own cousin. The records do not say if the local gendarmerie at Vouliagmeni received an official complaint of attempted rape in Kavouri that day. It would be surprising if they had. The young woman was unlikely to confess to the authorities that she had made a clandestine assignation with a married cousin, an admission which would place her well beyond the bounds of the strict moral code which controls most of Greek society.

Yet the fatal coincidence of Ann's death on 15 October revealed the liaison to anyone who cared to ask questions about it, everyone, apparently, except the police. They were supposed to be actively investigating a line of inquiry which stretched from a frustrated sexual encounter, even though there was absolutely nothing in the forensic evidence to support that theory. Fortunate coincidence, it would seem, had presented Major Goundras and the gendarmerie with a second sexual incident in Kavouri on the day in question and, far more significantly, with a man who could be swiftly identified. The strong resemblance of Moundis to the individual seen by the waiter and the petrol pump attendant, near the bus stop he later used to journey back to Piraeus, were sufficient grounds to make him a prime suspect for the murder of Ann. Yet he was interviewed at an early stage of the inquiry and set free, having established a sound alibi. Even after Moundis had been denounced by his wife, and Yannoulis had worked so assiduously to extract a confession, still nothing was made of the strange incident concerning the young woman. Before Moundis' arrest, as we have already seen, the British consul in Athens confidently assured Edward Chapman that the police were going about their work in exemplary fashion and had not changed their mind about the sexual motive, even though they still had no obvious suspect in mind. It was indeed extraordinary, if the attentions of the gendarmerie were so 'exemplary', how the testimony of witnesses concerning an apparent sexual attack in Kavouri on the same day Ann died could be so readily discarded. If the mysterious cousin was indeed Moundis, he also had good reason to keep quiet. Attempted rape was not a potentially attractive alibi in the circumstances of the Chapman case. It is probable, however, that Moundis was picked up a short time later because of this incident. It was unlikely that he convincingly lied himself out of it. Perversely, he had been presented with another original and convincing alibi.

In his own version of events, Moundis declared that after prowling about in the woods, he caught the Piraeus bus, alighting at Nea Faliron, near the football stadium. There he was fortunate to see his father-in-law, who gave him a lift. Moundis remembered the time he reached home, 10.30 p.m., because the cowboy serial 'Bonanza' was being screened on television. Dr Kapsaskis had established the time of Ann's death at about midnight that day, so Moundis was at home, having watched television, when Ann was being strangled. It seems that one of their frequent rows upset the household that evening. Moundis' wife was angry because she wanted to know where he had been and what he had been doing all day. Moundis' wife knew that her husband often went to Kavouri on his private missions – what Moundis described as his 'vice' – and she might have been forgiven for rushing off to the police as soon as the newspapers revealed the story of the 'terrible crime' committed there. Instead, she maintained silence for nine months.

After retracting the confession he had made to police at Piraeus, Moundis declared that he had been frightened when he read about the murdered woman being found at Kavouri – frightened because of his visit there that day and his fear of the police who knew all about his 'vice'. Fourteen years later, when I interviewed Moundis as a free but still officially unpardoned man on his old island home of Aegina, he employed considerable powers of invention to provide an account of what he had seen in Kavouri during the early evening hours of 15 October. Still adhering to the story of a chance acquaintance who had failed to keep her rendezvous, Moundis described entering the woods at, he thought, about 8.30 to 8.40. He heard footsteps behind him. At first he suspected 'a colleague' – someone else who would keep him company on the Peeping Tom patrol. Instead, he found himself confronting an unknown man who pulled a revolver. 'He told me he was a policeman and asked for my identity card. But I hadn't got it with me. Then he whistled two or three times and three other men came along.' Moundis was indeed facing a distinguished gathering in the dusky woods practically opposite the Pine Hill Hotel. He first recognized Yannoulis, the officer to whom he reported at Piraeus, and another officer from the same station, Captain Ioannis Liouneas. Another was a figure he quickly identified from 'pictures I had seen in the newspapers'. This was Charalambos Papadopoulos, brother of the ruling dictator, and much feared because of his role at the Orwellian 'Ministry of Public Security'. The fourth man, Moundis claimed, he was not sure about at the time, but later he identified him as Spyridon Michelis, director of security at Piraeus police HQ. Moundis says he gave the man with the revolver a false name and was brusquely told to clear off. Despite what should have been a disturbing experience, 'I stayed in the area because I was sick with my passion and this was a good place.' Moundis lingered a little further off, to see what might happen. He then described a scene in which all four men seized a girl who emerged from the hotel opposite. She was dragged, kicking and screaming, into a car which had been drawn up under the trees. Was he not unsettled by this scene? Moundis shrugged his shoulders: 'She could have been a prostitute, or something to do with drugs.' Everything in Moundis' past experience should have told him to shoot off with considerable speed once he saw Yannoulis, let alone the brother of the supreme dictator of Greece, in such circumstances. Yet he hung about in idle curiosity, watching for some action to compensate for his frustration.

Moundis' tale is a mixture of bravado and pure invention. In the first instance, neither Yannoulis nor Liouneas would have been deputed to mount a watch on the Pine Hill Hotel. Kavouri lay entirely outside their area of territorial responsibility, and neither was sufficiently senior to be included in an exercise involving, as Moundis later presumed, the kidnapping of a British journalist. If Moundis really had stumbled upon a group of desperados hiding in the undergrowth, they would have been plain-clothes figures from the Greek intelligence services. Moundis was insistent that Yannoulis and Liouneas were in uniform which, even for a half-hearted attempt at conspiracy, seems wildly provocative. Neither of the two officers from Piraeus police station recognized a convicted sex criminal who reported there regularly, which Moundis justified by citing the 'poor light'. It was, however, good enough for him to identify them, together with the brother of George Papadopoulos. Moundis shrugged again when I asked him if he really thought that three top brass officers and a VIP like Charalambos Papadopoulos would have been interested in a prostitute or 'something to do with drugs'. In fact, Moundis manufactured this entire episode in order to incriminate the two policemen and he threw in the brother of the dictator and the head of security at Piraeus simply to add weight to his claim. For the past fifteen years Moundis has damaged the credibility of all the attempts to clear his name by sticking to this fabricated business at Kavouri. His capacity to lie intricately has to be sieved from those parts of his testimony where he tells the truth. His lies sprang from the intense bitterness of facing the prospect of a lifetime behind bars. Yannoulis and Liouneas did indeed play a significant role in the story, but only after they arrested and then ensured the conviction of Moundis. The men Moundis claimed he saw did not murder Ann and nor were they anywhere near the Pine Hill Hotel at the time. Yet this fictional episode was not without some value. It helped Edward Chapman maintain interest and prolong the search for the truth when the Greek authorities were insisting that the case was finally and irrevocably closed. But Nicholas Moundis has never known who killed Ann, or why.

13 · A Duty to the State

> The concessions of the weak are the concessions of fear
>
> — Edmund Burke, MP for Bristol

Almost exactly ten months after the discovery of Ann Chapman's body, Nicholas Moundis was swept into the vortex of events which led to the claim by his lawyers that he was the 'Dreyfus of Greece'. Early on the morning of 8 August 1972, Moundis left for work as usual at a factory in the suburbs of Athens. At eight o'clock, he had a 'premonition' that he should return home and left almost immediately on the pretext of feeling unwell. More probably, he was reacting to long-felt suspicions. The Moundis home, rarely an oasis of domestic bliss, was shortly to erupt once again. Moundis surprised his wife ironing a pair of trousers belonging to a neighbour, a soldier in the infantry. On the table he saw two empty coffee cups, a packet of foreign cigarettes and a gold medallion. To Moundis the scene represented damning proof that his wife had been indulging in an insult to his manhood, something which no Greek male, even one so individually compromised as Moundis, could tolerate. He exploded with rage. 'I became very exasperated and began to beat her. I gave her many blows and left her unconscious.' As his wife cowered from his attack, she claims he screamed these fateful words: 'I'll make you like Chapman!'

Still blind with fury, Moundis stalked out of the house and

went straight to the home of his mother-in-law to complain about his wife's infidelity. He took the cigarettes and the medallion he had found on the kitchen table and flung them down in front of her. Moundis' mother-in-law kept her temper and implied that if his wife had found consolation elsewhere, Moundis had only himself to blame. He returned to work, still simmering.

Despite the many household rows, Moundis had gone too far this time. His wife was bent on revenge. Urgent conferences were summoned among the women of the family. One figure in this matriarchal circle, his wife's aunt, was destined to play a significant role in the developing crisis because, in Moundis' own words, 'she had an arrangement' with a policeman in Nea Faliron, the Athens suburb where she lived. In normal circumstances, the whole affair might have been dismissed as one of those upsets which frequently disrupt family life, but on this occasion events began to interlock in a manner which Moundis would find himself powerless to resist. The aunt gossiped to her policeman friend who listened with considerable interest to her account of all that had gone on in the Moundis household on the morning of 8 August. She left nothing out, including the angry outburst: 'I'll make you like Chapman!' The still unsolved murder of the young British girl found at Kavouri continued to rumble across the pages of Greek newspapers, where the theory that she had been the victim of a sex attack was still being firmly projected.

Nea Faliron is close to Piraeus and intelligence soon reached the police headquarters there, via the aunt's policeman friend, of the alleged incriminating words used by Moundis during the attack on his wife. The policeman who heard the tale knew all about Moundis, that he had been to prison for an assault on a young girl and that he often went to Kavouri in pursuit of his 'vice'. In the ten months which had elapsed since Ann's death, the police and gendarmerie forces had been unable to produce even one plausible suspect. Edward

Chapman's dismissal of the sexual theory and his angry claims of political conspiracy had not ceased. Bitter coincidence helped to snare Moundis. On 7 August – the day before the big row in which Moundis knocked his wife unconscious – Dorothy Chapman had sent off the letter containing the enormous bluff that she and her husband knew the identity of their daughter's killer, a letter which rocked the military establishment. As soon as word reached Piraeus police head-quarters that a man with a record of sexual crime had used highly suspicious words about Chapman during an assault on his wife, Moundis' fate was sealed. The perfect suspect had involuntarily thrown himself into the arms of the police, who had been perfunctorily instructed to 'solve' the crime in all haste. The aunt was called to Piraeus and told to repeat everything again – for money, Moundis would later claim. His wife was also summoned to provide her account and, Moundis insisted, also promised a generous bribe to sustain her story, especially the damning words invoking Chapman. Moundis himself was in innocence of all these developments, believing simply that he had taught his wife a lesson she would never forget. But on 27 August, his own long nightmare began with startling suddenness. At 1.45 p.m. officers from the local police station at Ayios Rendis arrived, without warning, at the factory where Moundis worked, arrested and handcuffed him and marched him off to solitary confinement. He knew that he was in serious trouble but had absolutely no idea why.

At seven in the evening on the same day, Moundis was fetched from his cell and ordered to sign the incident book. He was informed he would be charged with theft. Then he was handed over to the two senior officers who would interrogate him, Yannis Yannoulis, and his deputy, Liouneas. He was bundled into a police car which swept off to the main police station at Piraeus. Slumped between two officers in the back seat, Moundis sensed that the treatment he was getting was rather formidable for a petty business like theft, though he had no comprehension of what he was supposed to have stolen. Perhaps his wife had complained about the attack and he would now be accused of assault. This seemed a plausible explanation for his precipitate arrest at work and his subsequent treatment, including an entire afternoon in solitary confinement. At Piraeus, Moundis was shunted quickly up to the fifth floor of the main building where the security offices were situated. Moundis still insists that he was confronted there by the director of security, Spryidon Michelis, and again Charalambos Papadopoulos, the same men who in his account had been lurking in the woods outside the Pine Hill Hotel with Yannoulis and Liouneas. Michelis would undoubtedly be present at the interrogation of a man about to be accused of murder, but Yannoulis, in his version of events, never referred to the presence of the director of security operations at Piraeus, still less to the senior dictator's brother who controlled the Ministry of Public Order.

The account of what really happened at the Piraeus police headquarters has to be carefully filtered to detect fact from fiction. Moundis's record goes like this. As he entered the security office, someone said: 'We've brought him,' and then, 'That's him'. The interrogation was curt and to the point. 'On the evening of October 15th, 1971, when we found you at Kavouri, why did you give us false information?' Moundis replied that he'd been afraid because of his prison sentence, and the obligation he still had to report to the police. 'They said immediately that on that evening, when I was in Kavouri, I had killed – I said, "Not me, I have never done such a thing".' Then his account slips into effortless bravado. He, an unskilled labourer with a police record and every reason to cower before authority, shouted defiantly back at his interrogators: 'You did it – when you sent me away, I came back. I saw you forcing into a car a foreign woman who was shouting.' The effect of this accusation was evidently to turn

150

all four of his accusers 'a pale colour because they did not expect me to have seen them. And then they began negotiations'.

Confronted by the apparent collapse of their case, the four entered into detailed negotiations with the man who had now become their accuser. 'They told me they are the state and they do what they wish. They would say that I went to security alone because I felt remorse, and that they would be very good to me. They would sentence me to five years, they would give me 3 million drachmas on coming out of prison, they would look after my children.' But Moundis, suddenly the man of principle, would not comply. So he was again shut up in a small cell, this time with a piece of paper and a pencil, and instructed to ponder his future. Still he refused to confess. The hours passed and he was taken to another small room where torture commenced. Moundis then recounts how he was subjected to a series of assaults, including electric shocks applied to the genitals and hot, hard-boiled eggs lodged in his armpits. 'They put on my head a crown with screws and twisted it.' When he still refused to relent, he was dangled half-way out of a window in a prison sheet. 'Niko, your end has come. Better in prison than in the cemetery.' At this point, Moundis declares that he suddenly perceived the wisdom of signing a confession and quickly did so, though he had no idea what was actually written on the paper. Afterwards, his tormentors supplied lemonade and cake to help him recover.

In giving this account, Moundis is jolting in and out of the truth. He had already been questioned by the police over what he had been doing in Kavouri on the day that Ann died and had satisfied gendarmerie officers who were then leading the inquiry that he had a defensible alibi from his father-in-law. But he derived a continuing and dangerous frisson of excitement from having been in the area where such a sensational crime had been committed. It stirred his imagination, and that was why he threatened his wife with the words, 'I'll

BLOOD ON THEIR HANDS

make you like Chapman.' Significantly, he had not said 'I'll kill you – like Chapman,' as he might well have done had he actually been the murderer. Events began to happen more quickly: Moundis appeared in the highest court in the land charged with killing Ann; the police failed to produce any better proof against him than this single and far from compromising statement. But the family, and especially his wife and her aunt, had not lost the perfect opportunity to rid themselves of a man who was no longer wanted in his home.

All that Moundis described of his sudden detention at work and being plunged into solitary confinement at Ayios Rendis police station is correct. And it was there that he encountered Yannoulis who was to play a significant role in his conviction. In April 1985 Yannoulis eventually agreed to discuss Moundis and the Chapman case and we talked for almost four hours in the lobby of one of the big international hotels in Athens – 'neutral ground', Yannoulis called it. He told me about his long career as a policeman in a style that might have rolled from the lips of an inspector just retired from a Home Counties police force in England. Yannoulis was keen to give the impression of being a good, sound cop. Neatly-suited, manicured, portly and well-preserved for his sixty years, he rambled at length about his dedication to truth. He dismissed Edward Chapman as an exhibitionist who was interested only in the money he could get from dragging on with the story of his daughter's death. Chapman, he declared, had tried to get a thousand American dollars for a single appearance on Greek television, while he, Yannoulis, had never asked for anything and even suffered the indignity of having his own interview on the same programme slashed from fifty-five to two and a half minutes. He significantly avoided any mention of his own imminent appearance before a court in Piraeus. He had been accused of torturing a police suspect by the 'phalanx', beating on the soles of bare feet with, in this case, a cable. The suspect, a young anarchist, had struggled for five

152

years to prove his innocence on a charge of setting fire to a tax office. He, like Edward Chapman, encountered every kind of official prevarication in the fight for justice. The case reached court just two days before the expiry of the legal time limit. Yannoulis denied everything, insisting that the accused had injured himself by beating his own feet on the bars of his cell 'in order to defame the police'. Asked by the presiding judge why Yannoulis, who had prospered since the affair of Moundis, advancing to security chief at Piraeus, should risk his career in such a grubby business as torture, his accuser replied: 'He could never imagine that a victim of his would dare to denounce him to justice. That is why he moved around the room of tortures and gave orders.' In another eerie echo of the Chapman case, the head of the forensic service said he could not testify for sure whether the man's soles had self-inflicted wounds or bore the marks of torture. Yannoulis was luckier than Moundis. The jury cleared him on the charge of torture but found him guilty of illegally detaining the young man for five days. The final twist of the story was the ultimate revelation that the arsonist who had actually put a match to the tax office had long since been identified and confessed to the crime.

Yannoulis wanted to present the arrest of Moundis to me as a devastating act of detection, the culmination of a long career, a success so remarkable that it eclipsed all the efforts of those who had questioned Moundis and then released him for lack of evidence. But Yannoulis could not explain why, ten months after Ann's death, he suddenly hauled Moundis from work on suspicion of complicity in what the newspaper *Apogermatini* had called 'the crime of the last decade'.

'Moundis was off work so it seemed enough for me to investigate further,' was all he could say. And then: 'I caught him with honeyed words and sweet ways.' The 'sweet ways' which Yannoulis employed at the Ayios Rendis police station included prescribing the prolonged hiatus of psychological

153

uncertainty in solitary confinement. 'Then we told him we wanted to talk to him about some theft. We wanted to see what he would say. Later, I would bring in the business of what happened at Kavouri – but it was important that he, Moundis, should talk to us. That was clear.' The scene of the interrogation was then switched, as Moundis described, to the main police station at Piraeus, where Moundis was now confronted with the awful accusation that he had been involved in the death of Ann Chapman. 'Be careful, Nikos,' Yannoulis said to him, employing those 'honeyed words', 'be sure what you say.' Moundis at last seemed to burst with the desire to unburden his guilt. Yannoulis considered that his quarry was now ready to sign a statement of confession, and slid a sheet of paper in front of Moundis. 'He poured it out, we listened to him, we took it all down.' Moundis, said Yannoulis, began to see him just like a father. 'So I treated him in that way. I was gentle with him, just like a father.' Yannoulis' deputy, Liouneas, was also present at the confession and Moundis was made to repeat himself several times, so that there should be no misunderstanding. The statement was typed out and Moundis ordered to swear to it with his signature, and then repeat it again in front of the District Attorney. It is more than curious that Yannoulis and Liouneas – on the open admission of Yannoulis – did not sign the confession that Moundis had made. More than once during our long talk Yannoulis was at pains to point out that he and Liouneas had not signed the statement 'because it was not necessary' under Greek law. He had, of course, acted specifically on the information that had reached him from the policeman who had such an amicable 'arrangement' with Moundis' wife's aunt.

All the documentation connected with the arrest and interrogation of Moundis, including the alleged confession, has now disappeared from the public records. But in the period before he began manufacturing the tale about seeing

Yannoulis and the others in the woods at Kavouri, and then again in the security offices at the Piraeus police headquarters, Moundis supplied a far more accurate account of what transpired when he was brought into the company of Yannoulis for the first time. The examination commenced with Yannoulis saying: 'Moundis, we are reminding you that you killed the English girl.' Horrified, Moundis replied: 'My God, what are you saying!' He may also have manufactured the stories about torture – although such tactics were commonplace to enforce confessions at the time, and ill-treatment of accused prisoners remains an endemic problem in some quarters of the Greek police service today. Moundis was already quite sufficiently appalled at finding himself in the hands of the police, and particularly one man, Yannoulis. He was confronted with the 'evidence' that the formidable alliance of his wife and her aunt had accused him of admitting that he had killed Ann. Moundis also declares, with some conviction, that he was punched in the face and stomach, so that he vomited. He was taken to a nearby window, hung half-way out of it – 'better in prison than in the cemetery' – and then hauled back and given a sip of water. There was also softer treatment. If he would sign a confession admitting that he had killed Ann during a frustrated sexual attack, he would get a light sentence and money in the bank to help his family. Moundis was not the sort of man to put on a brave act in these circumstances. It may even be, given the promises which were made, that headline-making notoriety actually appealed to him until he realized, not long after making his confession, the appalling consequences.

The business of a promise of money has more than a ring of truth about it, because money did find its way, in peculiar circumstances, into a bank account opened in Moundis' name in Piraeus. This occurred while he was in the hands of the police. It is unusual, to say the least, for the police to permit those in their custody an opportunity openly to conduct financial transactions at a local bank. Yet Liouneas escorted Moundis, still in handcuffs, to the Piraeus branch of the National Bank of Greece. Liouneas had with him in a small briefcase several bundles of thousand-drachma notes – 22,000 drachmas, altogether. These were paid into an account especially opened in Moundis' name but he refused to sign for the payment, protesting greedily that he had been promised much more, at least 3 million drachmas. Liouneas, who had received a telephone call at the bank during the course of the transaction, answered: 'Didn't you see? They called me to the telephone and my bosses told me to pay this money in here and the rest in Switzerland.' Moundis, already beginning to suspect the integrity of the deal he had made, was left with no choice but to accept. Later the authorities tried to explain that the cash paid into the bank at Piraeus came from the proceeds of the sale of a television set and the wages Moundis was carrying when he was arrested. Even if that were true, and Moundis has lied about his visit to the bank with Liouneas, it was remarkably considerate of the police to permit a man who had just confessed to murder to sell his possessions and stroll out to deposit the proceeds.

Moundis had now signed his confession after a mixture of blandishment, threats and bribery. The next stage of the operation was to create a motive which would stand up in court and, more importantly, impress and silence Ann's parents. Yannoulis and Liouneas led Moundis carefully through the story he would tell. This went as follows: Moundis saw Ann waiting at the bus stop at St Nicholas and, finding himself attracted to her, created the opportunity for conversation. The introduction passed agreeably and Ann consented to step into the nearby field – about 200 metres back from the road. She placed her head in his arms and Moundis began fondling her body. All went well until the compliant Ann caught sight of Moundis' wedding ring and began to shout in protest at the prospect of sex with a married man. Moundis, in panic, then strangled her. A few variations were later introduced, including one that Ann began to resist only after Moundis tried to penetrate her pants and a tampon or sanitary towel with his hand. But the broad outline always remained the same: a young woman of impeccable character, finding herself with a few moments in hand while waiting for a bus, agreed to an interlude of casual sex with a complete stranger. The liaison was made despite a total language barrier. On 27 August and again the following day, Yannoulis and two other detectives escorted Moundis to the alleged scene of the crime. On neither occasion did anyone get out of the car. Yannoulis contented himself with pointing out the route which Ann took when she left the hotel for the bus stop and the location where the body was found. On the 29th Moundis was again taken by car to the scene and this time a minor reconstruction was enacted, Moundis being instructed to indicate how he climbed over the wall with Ann and precisely where they lay together. Yannoulis appeared satisfied by now that Moundis could be trusted to provide a thorough performance for the benefit of the public prosecutor, with the pathologist Kapsaskis and other key figures in attendance. This took place on 31 August. As is customary in Greece, the formal reconstruction was a well-publicized affair, with journalists liberally invited to attend and report on the proceedings.

Moundis went through his act mechanically. Ann was represented by a young police driver but private rehearsals in his cell at Piraeus featured a policewoman. 'She was about thirty,' Moundis told me when I visited him almost at the end of his long prison sentence. 'I was told I could touch her, fondle her breasts.' This was an example of how the authorities were cynically prepared to exploit Moundis, playing on his 'vice' as an incitement to appear convincing when the time came for a public display. Not everyone was satisfied with Moundis' performance that day at Kavouri. Even Kapsaskis, who now knew the details of the conspiracy, confided uneasily to several reporters that he 'wasn't happy'. Moundis seemed unsure whether he was supposed to be strangling or suffocating the figure who represented Ann. But it was David Bowen, the London pathologist brought in by Edward Chapman, who spotted severe inconsistencies when examining the photographic record of the re-enactment prepared by the police forensic department. He later wrote in the following terms to the Greek authorities:

> Whilst appreciating the difficulty of an accurate reconstruction of a crime, the action of the accused leaves some doubt as to the veracity of what actually took place. The sexual advance does not fit in with the fact that the deceased's pants were not disturbed. There is no evidence of strangulation in the reconstruction, the hands around the neck indicating suffocation, signs of which were not present at the post-mortem. The body dragged by the arms should reveal areas of abrasion there, rather than on the calves.
> . . . Although not a strictly medical matter, the removal of spiky wire from the fence would be difficult to carry out, without pliers and causing some damage to the accused's hands.

Small wonder that Kapsaskis was nervous, visibly fidgeting as Moundis went through his paces. He must have spotted one other glaring defect in the proceedings, also studiously noted by David Bowen. Moundis is left-handed. Kapsaskis' own post-mortem report had already concluded that the marks of strangulation on her neck were caused by the grip of a right hand. Later, when Bowen met Kapsaskis in Athens, Kapsaskis agreed that 'Moundis' reconstruction at the scene bore no relation whatsoever to the medical findings' although he insisted at the trial that he left the scene with the impression that the accused was the murderer.

Many of the journalists who were present left the scene filled with suspicion. Particularly observant among them was George Karageorges, who noted that Moundis was transported to and from the scene alone with Yannoulis, in a car driven by him. Karageorges, with others, was permitted to hear a tape-recording of Moundis making his confession. He told me: 'I have heard many such confessions – they are hesitant, worried, frightened, by disturbed people who are worrying what is going to happen to them. Yet Moundis speaks clearly as if he doesn't believe his own words.' Karageorges also cast an unusually professional eye over what he saw at Kavouri, as a judo expert who had examined the report of Kapsaskis with that experience in mind. To him, the report suggested that there was nothing clumsy about the killing of Ann, as the reconstruction by Moundis was supposed to prove. 'The killers of Ann knew that what they were doing would silence Ann permanently. It was an act carried out on the basis of experience.' Karageorges declared that he understood the 'unsavoury character' of Yannoulis, who was regarded by journalists in Athens as a junta supporter. When the Colonels fell in 1974 and Karamanlis the liberator arrived on the first day of freedom to take up residence in the Grande Bretagne Hotel in Syntagma Square, Karageorges was shocked to see Yannoulis among the police escort. 'What are you doing with that man at your side?' he called to Karamanlis. The man who became Justice Minister, George Manghakis, himself imprisoned by the junta, recalled Yannoulis sourly as 'one of the worst'.

In 1976, Yannoulis made an extraordinary outburst in an interview in the newspaper *Vraydini*. He abused Edward Chapman for coming from England to take away 'what is holy and sacred everywhere – legal authorities, security forces, the state, all are in shreds. In what other country is a legal decision disputed – nowhere in the world but here, in this place, Greece.' Of course, legal decisions are often the subject of dispute in any country where the judiciary is considered part of, and not above, the system of justice. But Yannoulis was required by his role in the Moundis affair to defend what he had done. 'I carried out my duty. I handed him over to the legal authority, which did what it had to do.' In performing that act of duty to the then illegal Greek state, he was nevertheless careful to ensure that his own signature did not appear on the confession statement. Yannoulis continued in the *Vraydini* interview: 'If her father is so filthy and miserable and wants his daughter's murderer – that sadist who strangled his daughter, God rest her soul, she wasn't to blame – to embrace and kiss him, he has that right.'

It is as well that Yannis Yannoulis and Edward Chapman have never met.

14 · Pandora's Box

Keep your head up! I am innocent.

— Nicholas Moundis

The trial of Moundis opened in the Athens criminal court on 5 April 1973 and lasted four days. By this time, Moundis had fully retracted the confession he had made to Yannoulis and company seven months earlier. In accordance with Greek law, Moundis found himself before four judges and four jurymen. Two of the judges – Potamianos, who was presiding, and Goltsis – were strongly identified with the regime. A third, Condelis, was known to have opinions firmly on the Right. The public prosecutor, Canellos, was considered a supporter of the junta. Moundis had by now withdrawn his 'confession' but there is no record in any case of that document being produced before the court. The defence rested on the alibi which had cleared him when he was first questioned by gendarmerie officers: Moundis had indeed been in Kavouri on 15 October, to meet a girl who failed to turn up. He caught a bus to Nea Faliron where he was picked up by his father-in-law, who would testify that Moundis was at home an hour and a half or two hours before midnight, the time established by Kapsaskis in his post-mortem as the probable moment of Ann's death. The defence attempted to demonstrate that if Moundis really had killed Ann, he must have committed the crime by about 8.15 in the evening, in order to be at Nea Faliron by the time he was seen by his father-in-law. But 8.15 is well short of midnight when Ann probably died and takes no account of Kapsaskis' finding that the body was moved between three and seven hours after death. To stretch the facts further to accommodate the prosecution case, Moundis would need to have stayed at the murder site until the early hours of Saturday morning, the 16th, moving the body around and scattering Ann's belongings in all directions. Even then, it is impossible to account for the fact, again recorded by Kapsaskis, that Ann had eaten some sort of small snack about an hour or an hour and a half before she died. The prosecution alleged that the fingerprints had been washed away by heavy rain which fell over the weekend of the 15th to the 18th. But, as the newspaper *Apogermatini* was later to record, this was not true. Other evidence was also quietly side-stepped, such as the absence of a struggle anywhere in the vicinity. The prosecution also deftly avoided any mention of the conclusions of Dr Kapsaskis that there were no signs of rape or even attempted rape.

After four days, all four judges and the four jurymen unanimously reached the verdict that Ann had been attacked by Moundis, punched in the face, knocked to the ground and strangled, tied at the wrists and ankles with the wire cut from a nearby fence, then dragged a short distance, the corpse being partially hidden with twigs, grass and two heavy boulders. This conclusion does not coincide at any point with the confession Moundis is supposed to have made to Yannoulis. The only consolation for Moundis was the decision of the court that he was guilty not of murder but of manslaughter in the course of attempted rape. This was a trifling consolation, since the verdict still carried a sentence of life imprisonment and Moundis could certainly expect this actually meant, under Greek law, a lifetime in captivity.

Dr Kapsaskis found himself in considerable difficulty when trying to adjust his own forensic findings to the case being assembled against Moundis. He even agreed that when Moundis had been taken to Kavouri to re-enact the crime, 'he did not display the usual emotion shown by even hard criminals'. Kapsaskis admitted that Moundis had never mentioned a struggle with Ann: 'He only said that as he put his hand in her lower part he felt a pad and the girl saw his wedding ring and became angry and resisted him, then he strangled her.' Had Moundis dragged the corpse about the field, scratches on the legs would have revealed that. Instead, the abrasions detected by Kapsaskis on the body indicated movement in a rather different manner. There were no fingerprints on the wire and no evidence of sperm to suggest ejaculation by Moundis. Having twisted his own evidence inside out, Kapsaskis declared that he still left the scene of the re-enactment 'with the feeling that he must be the culprit'. Journalists who were present remembered, however, his troubled uncertainty. Kapsaskis was firmly stuck, however, with the problem of the glaring discrepancies between these statements and the findings of his own post-mortem. He was left with no alternative but perjury. 'I certify that there must have elapsed one to one and a half hours from the moment the struggle took place to the moment of death and transfer of the corpse.' Now he was thoroughly compromised. The hour and a half supposed now to have elapsed between a 'struggle' and movement of the corpse synchronized even less well with the conclusion of Kapsaskis that Ann had eaten a small meal about an hour before her death. Movement of the body had now become instantaneous with death.

The second forensic expert, Ayoutantis, who assisted Kapsaskis at the autopsy, was next on the stand. He also wriggled uncomfortably with the facts but did not retract from his own original conclusion: 'The corpse must have remained at least three hours in its original position, maximum seven hours. There were various post-mortem marks on the body, due to the transfer of it after death.' No traces of blood were found under

Ann's fingernails, as might have been expected had she put up even a modest defence against attack, 'but perhaps they were washed away by the rain'.

The attention of the court then switched to the search conducted at the murder site and the curious ability of Ann's belongings to materialize at random. Demetrios Vallindras, another expert consulted by the gendarmerie, came to the court with a deeply troubled conscience which, he declared, he could no longer keep to himself. Together with a gendarmerie officer, Vassilakis, he had visited the site about ten days after the discovery of the body and found several pieces of a shirt, evidently cut with a knife and spotted with dried blood. These discoveries were handed to the police and then, like so much else, vanished. Moundis' lawyer, Theodoru, had no idea what had happened to them. 'I would have examined the blood group of those spots,' Vallindras told the court ruefully. He added: 'My conscience does not allow me to keep quiet about these findings.' The head of the criminologist service, Lieutenant Colonel Papadakos, was then questioned by Theodoru over the mysterious disappearance of the scraps of shirt stained with blood. Papadakos replied they had been 'discarded immediately because they were at least a year old'. From eighteen years' experience he knew 'perfectly well' what he should send for examination at the criminal laboratories and what he should not. He did not explain whether those years of experience permitted him to identify with absolute precision the age of linen, except to claim again the scraps were 'so old they had worms in'. Vassilakis, the expert in such matters, had mentioned nothing about worms and concluded reasonably that any material discovered stained with blood at the scene of a murder should be endowed with significance, and treated appropriately.

Edward Chapman sat grimly through the entire farce. 'The two doctors who gave evidence for the prosecution [Kapsaskis and Ayoutantis] could not even agree among themselves. I begged the court to call as witnesses various people from her party who had seen her on that last day, and also wanted the man who found the body [Hatzijannis] to be there. But I was overruled.' Chapman was then awarded the painful insult of one hundred drachmas for what he 'suffered because of the act of the accused against his daughter'. Moundis, on hearing the sentence of life for manslaughter, shouted from the dock to his parents: 'Keep your heads up! I am innocent.' Two officials from the British embassy also sat throughout the entire trial, evidently satisfied by this display of Greek justice. As the trial closed on 8 April 1973, it really did appear that the Chapmans would have to be satisfied that Moundis had killed their daughter in the course of attempted rape.

Chapman flew straight back from Athens to tell reporters in London that the trial had been blatantly rigged. He was already working closely with John Theodoru, Moundis' lawyer, who would represent his client for the next ten years without ever once asking for a single drachma for his services. Theodoru realized at the trial that he was confronting the formidable forces of the junta and that little could be achieved for Moundis – or Ann's parents – until democracy was restored to Greece. In April 1973, no one foresaw that within a year the Colonels would stumble to their ruin in Cyprus. Theodoru therefore settled down for a long siege. The difficulty confronting both him and Edward Chapman was twofold: first they had to overturn the conviction of Moundis and then they had to demand a fresh inquiry into who had really killed Ann. Theodoru now admits that he seriously underestimated the power of the forces at work behind the scenes. He himself suspected that Ann might well have been a courier or an agent with the sort of information which might threaten to compromise the military regime. Persistent reports that she was working for the CIA or even the USSR continued to circulate in Athens long after she was dead. Nevertheless, Theodoru remained convinced that his client would be freed by the first democratic government which

165

came to power. Once that breakthrough had been achieved, the way would be cleared for Edward Chapman, exploiting his status as *partie civile*, to demand a new inquiry into Ann's death. This was the thrust of all the attempts by Theodoru to secure an unprejudiced re-trial of Moundis.

The campaign was pushed ahead on two fronts. At the Chapmans' Putney home, an upstairs bedroom was rapidly converted into an office. Edward Chapman bought a second-hand typewriter at which he clattered away for hours, despatching letters all over the world to anyone who might remotely help in the battle. He schooled himself in forensic medicine, Greek jurisprudence, the principles of detection and international diplomacy. He assembled a bulging war-chest of documents connected with the case and sieved through it endlessly, hunting for the minutest scrap of evidence which might aid his theory of political conspiracy. Chapman exploited the press in London and Athens ruthlessly to keep the story simmering. 'I simply wouldn't have it that a small country like Greece could not be forced to give us the truth.' When the Colonels fell in 1974 and Karamanlis returned to power at the head of a government of national unity, he promptly received a letter from Chapman demanding that the Greeks re-open the case. The return post from Greece brought the first of many soothing replies from successive Karamanlis governments, but precious little in the shape of practical help or encouragement. Of course, if he could produce new evidence which might convince the courts of a miscarriage of justice, then the Greek authorities would be only too pleased to examine it. Until then, Moundis would remain in gaol for the manslaughter of Ann. Those who wished to conceal the facts gambled on the probability that an elderly and obsessive gentleman in Putney lacked the expertise and the power to lever open the sealed vault containing the truth.

Chapman applied constant pressure to consecutive ministers of justice. The reaction of one of them, George Stamatis, who was in office under Karamanlis from 1977 to 1980, was typical and, when I interviewed him in Athens in 1985, consistent. He told me through an interpreter that there were 'no problems with the Ann Chapman case – because it is closed'. He repeated the familiar rhetoric heard so often by Edward Chapman: every aspect of the case had been studied many times and Stamatis could not understand why Ann's father thought the decision unjust. Somewhat more remarkably, he held firmly to the view that judges and jurists during the time of the junta gave out 'just decisions'. Not once, he said, did the junta apply pressure on the courts or their decisions. Sitting comfortably behind an ample desk of his law office in the business district of Athens, Stamatis confidently assured me: 'People should be satisfied with justice in Greece.'

This touching faith in what happened during the years of the junta is shared by few others in Greece, and certainly not by Edward Chapman. Stamatis' immediate predecessor at the justice ministry was Constantine Stephanakis, who took office in Karamanlis' first government. There he was thrown immediately into contact with Edward Chapman and set the wheels in motion which eventually led to the hearing of the first appeal by Moundis. He also told me in 1985 that it was apparent to him that Ann Chapman knew 'certain things' and these were the reasons for her death. Stephanakis retained practically all his doubts and uncertainties about the case but could not accept that any democratic government, particularly one headed by Karamanlis, would stoop to concealing the truth. George Mavros, the old doyen of the liberal Centre Union Party, shared in the government with Stephanakis and regarded him as an honest man and a good lawyer: but in 1985, by which time he had seen the Centre Union Party collapse and its survivors, including him, receiving the full embrace of Papandreou's PASOK socialists, Mavros admitted his faith in Karamanlis had completely decayed. He had closed his mind to the opening of the 'Cyprus file' because it

167

was a Pandora's box from which terrible things might fly. 'There are also other people afraid,' Mavros told me, 'and although all parties agreed to open investigations, the actuality is always thwarted.' By lifting the stone concealing what had happened in Cyprus – and, for that matter, CIA involvement in the Greek military revolt – it was obvious that many other awkward creatures, like the truth about Ann, would wriggle out. The co-operation that Edward Chapman got from the Greek authorities following the restoration of democracy was always limited to the remarkable premise that the police, gendarmerie forces and the courts, all acting under the control of the junta, had been able to go about their work with complete detachment and honesty.

Early in 1975, Chapman fired his first important salvo since the collapse of the military regime by swearing a legal deposition at the Greek embassy in London, alleging that most of the evidence given at the trial of Moundis was false testimony. In April that year, Theodoru had formally lodged a notice of appeal by Moundis with the Supreme Court. Chapman had meanwhile located a formidable new ally in Professor David Bowen from Charing Cross Hospital. Bowen at once examined the report of the post-mortem by Kapsaskis and noted the tally of discrepancies between it and the case mounted against Moundis at his trial. Then, in May 1976, he agreed to fly to Athens for a face-to-face encounter with Kapsaskis at his home, at which the two men tried to reconcile those glaring inconsistencies. It was a long and tiring discussion and Bowen was disturbed because Mrs Kapsaskis insisted on being present. 'She should not, in my opinion, have been there,' he wrote to Chapman afterwards. The first point of dispute was the business of the body changing position after death. Kapsaskis tried to justify this to Bowen by proposing that 'the body could have moved due to the movement of the stones or a stone near it'. Bowen retorted that it was always unusual for dead bodies to move, particularly if they were bound hand and foot. Kapsaskis tried to evade the issue by suggesting that Bowen could not be absolutely sure – 'I said that I was, beyond practical doubt.' As the exchange continued, Kapsaskis agreed that what Moundis had re-enacted at the scene of the crime bore no relation at all to the medical findings. Mrs Kapsaskis intervened to propose that 'someone else' had made the comment attributed to her husband, that he left the field at Kavouri with the impression that the accused was the murderer: but Bowen retorted by quoting directly from the official record of the trial. In his account of the meeting he said: 'I found Dr Kapsaskis to be very crafty and cunning in trying to produce unlikely alternative theories as to how the body was moved. It only emphasized the fact that he altered his opinion, which would not look well in a court of law.'

Since that exchange, Kapsaskis has studiously avoided any further public comment on the affair. He has consistently refused to talk to me, except to say on the telephone, 'This business is over – for me, and for Greece.' Now enfeebled with age, Kapsaskis has retired to the coastal village of Sounion, where he apparently broods fitfully on his career. Many people in Greece have found it remarkable that in the wake of the collapse of the military regime, he was never asked to account for his services to the Colonels.

Another key figure who remains silent is Ayoutantis, who also worked on the post-mortem and had difficulty in keeping up with Kapsaskis' rapid changes in tack during the first Moundis trial. When a researcher asked if he would be willing to meet me in Athens, he replied over the telephone: 'I'll meet once – but only to say goodbye.'

Bowen himself has one curious memory of his mission to Greece. Leaving his hotel for a stroll one evening he was intercepted by several Greeks who swept him off to a basement and plied him liberally with ouzo, for which they later demanded a large sum of money. During his period as an involuntary guest, the professor was told that he would be

169

'taken to Mr Chapman'. That evening out in Athens cost Bowen £300 in travellers' cheques.

Theodoru's hopes for the re-trial were pinned to a large extent on the expert style of Bowen's analysis of the Kapsaskis post-mortem. But he had also visited the prison on the island of Aegina where Moundis was held prior to his first trial, and spoken to prisoners who had been held there with him. Liouneas, the detective from Piraeus, had claimed at the trial that Moundis had boasted of killing Ann almost as soon as he walked through the gates of the prison. Since the original plan to use the induced confession had collapsed, the police had been forced to seek corroboration of his guilt elsewhere: but Moundis' fellow-prisoners at Aegina assured Theodoru that the police story was a fabrication. Moundis had shouted his innocence to anyone who would listen. Contact with other prisoners had in any case been restricted by isolating him in solitary confinement.

When the judges at last sat, the prospects at first seemed promising. Out of the seven who would reconsider the evidence, only two could be clearly identified as sympathetic to the former military regime. The overwhelming bias remained to the Right but at least one left-of-centre judge had been included on the panel. The verdict, when it came, was therefore a crushing disappointment. The appeal was lost by four votes to three. Edward Chapman received the news stoically. Despite the weariness of waging a fight for the truth for almost seven years only to see his hopes dashed yet again, Chapman told the press that he would never abandon the struggle 'against this deception and cover-up'. The promulgation handed down by the Supreme Court declared that the appeal had been rejected because of the lack of 'any new evidence' – repetition of the familiar theme. Edward Chapman's frustration boiled over. The evidence proving that Moundis could never have killed Ann had always been staring the judges in the face, in the shape of the gulf which separated the findings of the post-mortem performed by Kapsaskis and Ayoutantis, and the subsequent crude attempts by the prosecution to squeeze the facts to fit the conviction of Moundis. Chapman was by now entirely sceptical about all Greek expressions of sympathy and offers of help. His conviction of a political conspiracy was deeper than ever but there seemed little prospect of mounting a determined assault on those centres of power in the Greek state occupied by men determined to keep the truth from him.

In 1980, however, a fresh glimmer of hope appeared. The New Democracy party, the creation of Karamanlis which had ruled Greece since the return to democracy, was toppled in the general election by Andreas Papandreou's Pan-Hellenic Socialist Movement. Vast crowds thronged Syntagma Square in the centre of Athens proclaiming yet another revolution. At home in Putney, Edward Chapman observed events in Greece with considerable interest. Now that the Left had at last won power, he reasoned that he might exploit their bitter ideological hatred of the Colonels to launch a fresh attack. At first, the bland sophistries of Papandreou's government matched those of the previous conservative regime. There was one important difference in emphasis. The new occupant of the justice ministry was George Manghakis, himself a former political prisoner of the Colonels who had experienced the rigours of secret and crude interrogation. Publicly, Manghakis repeated the ritual creed concerning the necessity to separate his essentially political powers of state from the sacred independence of the Greek judiciary. This was a familiar theme, constantly hummed by the stream of justice ministers who had passed before Chapman. In private, however, Manghakis offered Ann's parents considerable advice and encouragement. When the eminent British barrister Fenton Bresler visited Athens to discuss the case with Manghakis, the minister freely told him that he could 'draw what conclusions he wished' from the fact that when the second application for the re-trial of Moundis came before the Supreme Court his own chief prosecutor recommended to the presiding judge that it should succeed. Manghakis was delicately conceding that ministers of justice could, after all, have some influence over the machinery of the nation's legal system. Bresler was not particularly impressed. He told Manghakis bluntly that in Britain it would be unthinkable for Moundis to go to prison on such thin evidence. The five judges of the Supreme Court who sat to hear the case of Moundis for a third time did not agree. The second application for a re-trial was again dismissed, this time by the considerable margin of four to one.

Aspects of this decision are intriguing. Legal minds in Athens could identify only one judge out of the five known for his junta sympathies. But in the few days before the court sat, the legal machinery underwent some interesting adjustments. The appeal was due to be heard by a penal department of the Supreme Court, headed by a distinguished and respected judge, Constantin Stassinos. At the last moment, instructions came from the public prosecutor that the case would instead be switched to another penal division, headed by the equally respected Basil Lenardos. His coterie of judges was considered, however, to include a number who had enjoyed 'connections with the junta'. The suggestion of last-minute manipulation to get the right result might be overstated, but given the slender majority against appeal at the first re-trial, the outcome surprised many seasoned legal observers in Athens, among whom it had been confidently anticipated that Theodoru was about to win his long campaign on behalf of Moundis.

Edward Chapman trudged back to the airport in defeat yet again, now seventy-eight years old, his savings exhausted, and still no nearer the truth about his daughter's fate. It was almost ten years to the day since Moundis had been convicted of Ann's manslaughter. Edward Chapman's sense of acute disappointment is easily judged from this note he sent to Manghakis:

> By this decision of four men, Greece is bearing the terrible burden of them and the military junta judges of the trial court of April 1973 . . . but where does this leave me after eleven and a half years' fight for the truth of things? Am I to be denied my fundamental rights to be given the answers to many questions asked of the military dictatorship, the New Democracy government and the present socialist government?

Yet all was not completely lost. I had been following the case of Ann for some years in the British press and in 1982 I wrote to Edward Chapman advising him of the little-known right he enjoyed as an EEC citizen to petition the European Parliament for redress of a grievance against an authority or authorities in another member state of the European Community. Chapman seized the chance, however slight, to continue the battle: 'For the first time in twelve years the struggle to find the truth is out of Greece.' The Petitions Committee of the Parliament, sitting in Brussels, patiently considered the unique proposition that it should challenge the highest legal authority in a Community member state. The vote was narrowly in favour of commencing an inquiry in the hands of a member of the Parliament. The motion seemed destined to be lost until a Greek New Democracy deputy, the Athens lawyer, Costas Gontikas, first declared his intention to abstain and then fired the conscience of the committee with the declaration that majority opinion in Greece lay in favour of Edward Chapman and the innocence of Nicholas Moundis. His speech persuaded one voluble, but in this case, crucial, Italian Communist MEP, Angelo D'Sante, to switch his vote in favour of an inquiry. The Danish chairman of the committee ordered the immediate commencement of work, in my hands.

15 · When the Fleet comes in

The hand that signed the treaty bred a fever

— Dylan Thomas

The seed sown by Spiro Agnew during his visit to Athens in October 1971 was a flourishing sapling three years later, with fruit already ripe for the picking. Some in fact had already been sampled. The nuclear-armed American Sixth Fleet now enjoyed secure port facilities near Athens, putting an end to at least one source of White House anxiety about security in the eastern Mediterranean. There remained the perennial problem of Cyprus. To American eyes, practically everything which happened on the troubled island seemed capable of blowing the whole region apart, sending out sparks which could ignite further dangerous fires on Middle Eastern shores. In the ten years since Dean Acheson had conceived the plan to put the carving knife to Cyprus, the situation had continued to deteriorate. The Americans were sure about one thing: there was going to be no second Cuba in the Mediterranean. Secret traffic channelled back from the US embassy and the CIA post in Nicosia alerted Washington from 1973 onwards to the alarming possibility that Archbishop Makarios was falling under Soviet influence. It was certainly true that Makarios had been receiving clandestine arms shipments from Czechoslovakia, which on one occasion led to a full-scale gun battle when the old Enosis warrior, Grivas, tried to snatch them from Reserve Guard officers loyal to Makarios. The CIA had the Cypriot head of state — whose writ was in fact confined to the Greek cantons — firmly marked as pro-Russian and pro-Arab.

There were other pressures on the Americans. From Tel Aviv, the Israelis were urging Nixon to do something about the turbulent priest, preferably eliminate him, before the Soviets had the chance to found a Cuban-style military colony on the island which could then pose a running threat to every strategic air- and sea-route in the region. The United States was by now thoroughly intoxicated with the notion that time was not on their side in Cyprus. Using NATO meetings as cover — practically the only forum where Greeks and Turks sat at the same table — Washington indulged in the pretext of posing as mediator between the two sides over the future of the island. The chances of any amicable agreement between Athens and Ankara, without the application of persuading forces, was always so remote that policy-makers at every level knew they were indulging in a charade. In reality, the Americans had begun to tell the Greeks from 1973 onwards that future aid and comfort for the junta would depend entirely upon their good behaviour over implementation of some version of the Acheson plan, as updated by Agnew during his visit to Greece in October 1971. The CIA remained pleasantly surprised that the content of the former Vice-President's mission had remained secret, due in the largest part to the warm spirit of co-operation which existed between the American, British and Greek intelligence systems. What now supplied the situation with additional urgency was the rapidly disintegrating internal political fabric of Greece itself. In short, the country, together with the rule of the Colonels, seemed to be falling apart. Ambassador Tasca had long been troubling Washington with reports of internal divisions within the junta. The longer Greece remained politically flexible to American pressure, the easier it would be to impose a solution in the matter of Cyprus.

The uprising at the Athens Polytechnic in November 1973 detonated all these cherished hopes. The fuse which had lit this explosion was a memorial demonstration commemorating the fifth anniversary of the death of the old premier, George Papandreou. Many arrests were made by the police and although the subsequent trial witnessed an unusual display of leniency by the junta-controlled courts, fresh trouble was brewing. Students from the main polytechnic, who had used the Papandreou commemoration to signal to the world a message of freedom, began to make provocative demands for elections to their own unions. This was highly combustible material at a time when Papadopoulos had greater need than ever to demonstrate his mastery over the country and the rival elements within the junta. He first made the mistake of sending emissaries to negotiate with the students and then, when that exercise failed, began to make threats. The students responded with a gigantic assembly at the polytechnic at which they unfurled banners hurling insults at the dictatorship, demanding 'bread, freedom and an end to fascism'. The gathering quickly evolved into a self-propelled soviet among the Athens students. Amid the wild euphoria which rapidly developed in those November days, student leaders convinced themselves that their dramatic demonstration could wreck the rotten edifice of the junta. They had no comprehension of the cynical manipulation of the event by Ioannides, who despatched *agents provocateurs* to the scene as part of his long-gestating design to oust Papadopoulos. Proof that Ioannides' private gestapo had mingled freely with the students was supplied in 1975 at the trial of those responsible for the bloodshed which followed the government's decision to quell the unrest.

At about 7.30 p.m. on 16 November, at which time a huge throng had gathered within the polytechnic grounds, the police began firing shots, they claimed into the air, but, as hundreds of witnesses later declared, in fact straight into the mass of bodies before them. The regime would later claim that twenty-seven were killed. The real figure, published only after the junta had fallen, was forty-three. Among those who testified to a limited tally of only twenty-seven fatal victims was Dr Dimitrios Kapsaskis.

Papadopoulos was left with every remaining shred of his credibility in tatters. He tried to extricate himself by accusing exiled politicians of stirring up unrest, feeding what he called the rabid anti-American fervour of anarchists and communists who were exploiting the polytechnic students. Although Papadopoulos did not yet accept it, the sack of the polytechnic had finished him before his peers in the junta and, far more significantly, those at the American embassy. Towards midnight on 24 November 1973 a convoy of armoured vehicles arrived at his private residence. He was smartly saluted by an officer who handed him his own resignation statement. Tanks and armoured cars prowled the streets of Athens while the morbid farce was carried to its conclusion. At dawn, Greece woke up to another dictator, though few had ever heard of the obscure General Phaidon Gizikis who now addressed the nation on the radio as the new saviour of the revolution. Ioannides had chosen to avoid the errors of overexposure which led Papadopoulos to his downfall. The pathetic and irrelevant figure of Gizikis merely initialled the decrees which Ioannides handed down.

All informed sources of opinion both in and outside Greece saw the hand of the United States and especially the CIA in the abrupt dismissal of Papadopoulos. They were right. Papadopoulos' usefulness evaporated after the draconian measures taken against the students at the polytechnic. His misjudgement also conveniently handed the Americans an opportunity to manipulate a change in direction. The pressure exerted on the regime to co-operate in the matter of Cyprus had been virtually unrelenting since Agnew's mission in 1971. In mitigation, Papadopoulos had always pleaded the difficulties of fuelling any kind of insurrection on the island, as a pretext to permit the Turks to annexe their share. The army, representing the collective national consciousness of Hellenism, would always have leapt at the opportunity to achieve even partial Enosis; but the navy, the source of smouldering resentment, and insurrection, against the regime, posed a problem which Papadopoulos could not resolve. Even his own modest political faculties foresaw that adventures in Cyprus promised disaster, no matter what promises the Americans and the CIA might care to make. To the United States, military regimes like that in Greece were transitory affairs in the greater game of geo-political engineering; but the Greek Colonels were preoccupied with a narrow and national obsession with survival. Papadopoulos had not demurred at external machinations against Makarios and was even prepared to contemplate assassination: he had sent Grivas to Cyprus with the same motives that led the Germans to permit the export of Lenin to Moscow in a sealed train. If revolt could be fermented within, the aims of the 'national centre' in Athens – and Washington – could be accomplished without compromise to the security of the regime in Athens. After the revolt and bloodshed at the Athens Polytechnic, the message was clearly understood in the White House that Papadopoulos had served his time. The resignation statement thrust into his hands in the small hours of 25 November 1973 was a notice to quit drafted in and dictated from Washington.

Papadopoulos instantly deduced that Ioannides was not the guiding hand behind the coup. He was now a prisoner of the regime he created simply because the CIA had abandoned him. Preparations for the event had been in hand for weeks. Yet the streets of Athens had been filled with tanks, armoured cars and soldiers without a single word leaking to him as head of the Greek state, and also of course the principal

178

victim. Papadopoulos had been warned in the wake of the polytechnic massacre that he was now in serious trouble with his former benefactors. But he deluded himself into believing that he had succeeded in appeasing the Americans by laying responsibility for the whole affair on communist sympathisers within the student movement. This was, in fact, another clumsy and, as it proved, costly blunder. To the White House, it seemed that Papadopoulos had tacitly recognized the presence of powerful anti-American sympathies in the country, which in turn could shine searchlights on American complicity in the original 1967 coup against Constantine. The spectacle of the police and troops ruthlessly quashing unarmed students chanting slogans against American bases in Greece thoroughly rattled Washington. The CIA therefore moved quickly to ease Ioannides effortlessly into power.

What happened in the months between the student revolt and the collapse of the junta in 1974 remains a dark chapter in the history of Greece, because of the obstinacy displayed by Karamanlis and his successor, Andreas Papandreou, against opening 'the Cyprus file'. The parliamentary inquiry which commenced in 1986 bore all the hallmarks of mere lip-service to the election pledge made by Papandreou. Yet a close study of the events which followed the collapse of the junta can be used to throw some patches of light into the gloom. Ioannides was the obedient proxy of the Americans when they ordered the operation to divide Cyprus in July 1974. The elimination of Makarios was crucial to success. The grand design worked but only just, because the 'clerical Castro' in fact escaped with little more than a few singes to his episcopal raiment. Ioannides was subsequently charged with complicity in the attempted assassination of the Cypriot head of state, yet the trial was abruptly dropped on orders from Karamanlis, after consultations with opposition leaders, including Andreas Papandreou. The phrase employed in a government decree was suspiciously revealing: Ioannides was let off the Cyprus hook to avoid 'a possible disturbance of the country's international relations'. The foundation of that statement was a warning from Ioannides that he would not hesitate to use the trial as a public platform to broadcast to the world everything he knew concerning American manipulation of the junta. He would also let off fireworks over the tragedy in Cyprus. Karamanlis was thus forced to yield to pressure from President Gerald Ford to drop all charges against Ioannides in connection with Cyprus. Later, in September 1975, Ford also moved to halt a budding congressional probe into the activities of the CIA throughout the whole duration of the Greek and Cyprus drama.

Many Democrats who had consistently opposed America's succour for the Greek military regime had detected the broad outlines of the Cyprus plot even before Ioannides despatched his 'angel of death', Nikos Sampson, to liquidate every Turkish Cypriot on the island. In one amazingly obvious move, the deputy assistant secretary of state and an old hand with Greek and Cypriot policy, Rodger Davies, had been despatched as ambassador to Nicosia early in July 1974, just days before the bloodshed began. Davies was drafted in to run the CIA operation on the spot once Cyprus had been carved in two. The escape of Makarios signed his death warrant. Within a month of arriving in Cyprus, Davies was murdered by agents of the Archbishop ticking off the scorecard of revenge.

Meanwhile, American manoeuvring began to encompass Turkey, where a new government formed in January 1974 held out the prospect of an attractive re-alignment of interests. The new Prime Minister, Bulent Ecevit, enjoyed two happy distinctions. First, he had studied Greek at university, and secondly, he had once been a pupil at Harvard of Henry Kissinger, now the American Secretary of State and the most important enthusiast for the plan to settle outstanding problems in the region by dividing Cyprus. Ecevit had one other

180

important qualification which commended him to the Americans: like Karamanlis, still brooding in Paris but now sensing that the portents indicated his imminent return to power, Ecevit regarded Cyprus as an irrelevent distraction which should be relegated as quickly as possible in the wider interests of *détente* between Greece and Turkey.

In February 1974 Ecevit advanced a federal solution to the Cyprus problem during an address to the Turkish Parliament. He broke no new ground in so doing, because variations on a federal theme had been integral to the philosophy of most Turkish governments for the best part of a century. But in even raising the issue he took risks with his own political survival as the head of a potentially unstable coalition. Ecevit had been secretly briefed on American plans for the island and knew that the Greek dictators would shortly be lured to their doom in the course of an adventure designed to offer Turkey, as one of the three guarantor powers of an independent Cyprus, the opportunity to mount an intervention unchallengeable under international law. Ecevit's long-term plans for *détente* with Athens required a new regime headed by Karamanlis. Professor Nicholas Devlotoglou, the right-wing radical who has long been a scourge of the Greek socialist establishment, advanced the proposition in an article in *The Times* in December 1984 that Ecevit had attended clandestine meetings with Karamanlis at Marne, a small town just outside Paris, during which they reached a secret accord to resolve all the outstanding issues of dispute between the two countries. Devlotoglou gave the clear impression that the secret summits had taken place with the benevolent encouragement of the United States, and that both Karamanlis and Ecevit had been instructed on what was about to transpire in Cyprus.

The explosive charge that Karamanlis was central to the conspiracy with the Turks also finds an echo in memories of the period by George Mavros, who told me in 1985 that

Cyprus was the 'Watergate of Greece', certain ultimately to consume the reputation of Karamanlis. Mavros took office as Foreign Minister in the first liberation government formed by Karamanlis while he was still clutching together the rapidly dispersing elements of his Centre Union Party. He asked the imprisoned Colonels about the objective of their attack on Cyprus and what they had intended their next move to be. 'They replied that they did not know.' Their nonchalance struck him as breathtaking. Mavros rapidly became convinced that the Americans were behind the idea to settle the Cyprus issue by dividing the island, which then posed the question of just how much Karamanlis had known about the plot. He had returned from Paris to preside over the restoration of democracy brimming with promises to hold a full inquiry over what had happened in Cyprus and who was responsible. Yet within months, all charges of complicity against Ioannides, who armed Sampson and his piratical crew, had been dropped completely. In Parliament, Karamanlis resisted all attempts to 'disturb the international relations of Greece' by opening the file on the episode and continued to do so throughout his premiership and his later tenancy of the presidency. Mavros told me the Americans had warned Karamanlis of the dangerous consequences of opening the file 'and Karamanlis was definitely against it because he had great responsibilities'. By 1977, the electoral tide had ebbed strongly away from New Democracy, the party Karamanlis founded to guide Greece through the rough waters of the restoration of democracy. He therefore quickly arranged his own elevation to President in order to maintain a position on the bridge where he could continue to control the destiny of Greece once the inevitable occurred in the shape of electoral victory for Papandreou's socialists. During this period, the growing disenchantment felt by Mavros for Karamanlis turned to complete disillusion and then political divorce. Mavros escorted the remaining fragments of the old centralist liberal grouping into coalition with Papandreou. In so doing he abandoned virtually all his credibility with the Greek electorate, while Karamanlis mostly preserved his own intact. In saying that Karamanlis had 'great responsibilities' over Cyprus, Mavros elegantly skirts around the fact that before the charges against Ioannides over complicity in the Cyprus coup were abruptly dropped, Papandreou, as an important opposition leader, had also been consulted and given his approval. When Papandreou won power at the general election in 1980, he repeated all the hoary old promises about opening the Cyprus file but, once in office, displayed no more eagerness than his predecessor to do so. I asked Mavros, now long out of government, how he could account for that and he replied that he had given up bothering to press Papandreou on the issue because he knew what the answer would be.

Throughout the early months of 1974, the great design over Cyprus moved inexorably towards its conclusion. The Americans were assisted by several breaks of good fortune – among them the death of Grivas who, as an unreconstructed advocate of total Enosis, could be relied upon to subvert any scheme which fell short of that. The arrival in power in Ankara of Bulent Ecevit promised full co-operation from the Turks. In January, Nikos Sampson went to Athens for talks with the local CIA controllers and had one especially rewarding encounter with a visitor from Cyprus, the former head of the CIA station in Nicosia. At the same time, a carefully managed exercise in 'destabilization' was taking place in the waters of the Aegean, as Greece and Turkey hurled insults at each other over their respective territorial rights. By early summer, relations between Athens and Makarios in Nicosia had plunged to zero. Makarios branded the leaders of the 'Union with Greece' EOKA–B movement as nothing short of Greek military agents. During the first few days of July, Makarios became sufficiently alarmed about rumours of an impending coup staged by Ioannides to send a toughly worded 'hands off' letter to Athens. He summarized his feelings at the time when he later wrote: 'I have sensed, and sometimes almost felt, an invisible hand reaching out from Athens and seeking to terminate my earthly existence.' Makarios did not know that the date on which the independence of Cyprus would end – together with his 'earthly existence' – had already been selected as 15 July. The final communication between the Colonels and the Turkish government had been exchanged at the NATO summit in Brussels late in June, when Ecevit himself had been present, together with the message carrier for Ioannides, the then Greek premier Androutsopoulos. The Americans, who so greatly feared the outbreak of war in the eastern Mediterranean, were now actively provoking war – in the cause of peace.

Of course, since all the strings were pulled from Washington, with additional manipulation from local CIA stations, the risk of actual conflict between the respective national forces of Greece and Turkey was entirely notional. The Greeks have a special word for such an elaborate pretence, 'skevoria', a good deal of which was employed during the build-up to the coup. A full disclosure was made to the British government which, apart from retaining an incurable loathing for Makarios acquired during his long insurrection against imperial power, remained a key factor in the Cyprus equation through its role as a guarantor of the national settlement and possessor of the two key sovereign bases. Neither the British nor the Americans could foresee the situation of almost comic irony which would arise when Makarios managed to evade Sampson's lynch mob and escape aboard a British helicopter. Sampson was smuggled on to the island some days before the rising, while a handful of selected officers from the Greek-officered National Guard had already visited Athens to hear of their 'historic mission' from the lips of Ioannides himself. On the morning of the 15th, the Cypriot National Guard moved, under the command of Sampson, and shots were fired at the Presidential Palace where Makarios was addressing a group of schoolchildren. Sampson never managed to correct the bungle he made at this crucial stage of the operation, despite chasing the Archbishop all over Cyprus. Makarios escaped, his palace in flames. In Athens, Ioannides raged and screamed, demanding 'the head' of his elusive victim. Sampson declared himself President, amid the tempest he had unleashed. Greek and Turkish Cypriots were plunged into a terrifying pogrom, as all the bonds of restraint within the island shattered in an instant. Just how many died during the seven nightmare days has never been correctly established. Entire villages were put to the torch, the throats of men, women and children slit. In the Turkish zone, the authorities now maintain as national shrines those grisly pits where the occupants of complete communities were buried in mass graves. The scale of the inter-communal fighting came as an unexpected shock to the Americans, and perhaps even to the Turks who had assembled their 'invasion force' in a string of ports along the Anatolian coast. On the 19th, Turkish naval forces were at sea and close to Cyprus. At dawn the following day, the first unopposed landings were made and by the 20th each initial Turkish objective had been secured. The ceasefire, established under American 'pressure', demonstrated the willingness of Turkey to comply with her secret obligations.

While the Turks continued to insist – correctly, in international law – that they were exercising powers of intervention granted by the Treaty of Guarantee, the Greeks had been branded marauders who had broken into the island, tried to murder the President and then loosed the dogs of civil war. Ioannides was convinced that the CIA had double-crossed him by conniving in some way at the seemingly miraculous escape of Makarios. He also refused to believe the Americans would restrain the Turks from using the massive force of well over 40,000 troops they had now landed on the island to secure a permanent presence from which they could never effectively be dislodged. Greece, and not Turkey, appeared in the eyes of the world as the architect of naked aggression, a situation which constituted a vast reservoir of danger to the survival of the military regime in Athens. No wonder Ioannides is said to have railed at Joseph Sisco, America's roving peacemaker, when he turned up in Athens at the height of the crisis: 'You fooled us.' The Greeks had so far achieved nothing from '*skevoria*', not even the promise of partial Enosis in the form of a share of the spoils they expected to claim over the coffin of Makarios, because Makarios was alive and well and damning Ioannides all the way from London to the UN in New York. In fact, the escape of the Archbishop was a setback to everyone who had a hand in the affair. The Americans, Greeks, British and Turks – not to mention others watching from the sidelines – all much preferred a dead Makarios. In a give-away statement made as the crisis began to cool, Henry Kissinger conceded that the Archbishop's return to power in Cyprus was 'certainly not excluded'. The Americans were inadvertently conceding that they had the power to decide his fate. For a man they were so keen to brand as the potential red demon of the Mediterranean, this represented a remarkable change in attitude and very few observers saw it otherwise; but the fact was that there could be no second attempt on Makarios' life. Ioannides, meanwhile, blundered from one disaster to the next. Demented with anger and frustration over what he saw as American duplicity, he first tried to call a chaotic mobilization for war against Turkey and, when the impotence of that gesture became clear, then despatched a Commando force aboard fifteen transport planes to seize Nicosia. This operation, staged on the night of 21 July, was a complete fiasco. In this single engagement of Greek forces during the entire Cyprus episode, four planes were shot down and the remainder returned in humiliation to Athens, troops still aboard. The Americans observed this charade with an attitude of

186

detached satisfaction, confident that, if left to himself, Ioan-nides would continue to overplay his hand magnificently. In Paris, Karamanlis was preparing for the summons he had been alerted would shortly come to return to Athens.

There have been few patriots in history who returned, as did Karamanlis, to an ecstatic welcome which included representatives of the military regime he was about to replace. He later wrote: 'Never was I calmer, never did I have the situation more under control.' In the previous twenty-four hours, Karamanlis, like de Gaulle before him, extracted every ounce of drama from his role as the reluctant saviour. In fact, the Athens rumour-machine had been buzzing for days with reports of his imminent return. It served many interests, some of them surprising, to stimulate the growing conviction that the days of the junta were drawing to an end. As the appointed date for the coup in Cyprus approached, the Soviet embassy in Athens, eager to signal protectively its own privy knowl-edge of the affair, contacted a Turkish radio correspondent, Cem Besar, and asked him to drop in 'for a friendly chat over a coffee'. There, Besar was fed with the story that Ambassador Tasca and Joseph Sisco had been meeting with Karamanlis secretly in Paris. This was a provocative gesture, intended to inform Ankara that Moscow knew very well that the fate of the junta had been sealed. Without doubt, the open channel on internal resistance politics established by Arne Treholdt at Papandreou's Stockholm headquarters supplied the Russians with all they wished to know about events in Greece and Cyprus. Russian acquiescence also showed itself in another form, when Gerald Ford and Leonid Brezhnev agreed during a meeting in Vladivostok that the situation created by the Turkish intervention was 'acceptable' to both superpowers. Not long afterwards, just before the abortive 15 July move against Makarios, Besar observed another hint of forth-coming dramatic change. He saw a large number of station-wagons in a main street near the city centre, stacked with placards and posters featuring the returning hero, Kara-manlis. Besar, who is now based in northern Cyprus reporting for one of the largest Turkish dailies, told me: 'We all knew what was going on.'

Ioannides was certainly not going on, even though early steps taken against him seemed no more than a mild rebuke. He was despatched on six months' discretionary leave from the army. Before the prison doors finally slammed on Ioannides, there was one last act in the unfolding drama of Cyprus. The conference of guarantor powers summoned in Geneva was interrupted by the apparently disturbing news that Turkish troops in Cyprus had once again commenced an advance. Within a few hours they had reached their target, the so-called Attila Line, which had been the objective from the moment intervention began. All further movement then ceased. The Turks now occupied roughly 40 per cent of the island, including a large chunk of the capital, Nicosia. Kissinger issued assurances that the Turks would seek no further territorial gains, an assurance he was evidently able to supply with absolute conviction. Karamanlis, of course, voiced the inevitable outrage of every Greek; but, in reality, the task of re-invigorating Greece after seven years of military misrule presented Karamanlis with quite sufficient domestic preoccupations. Cyprus was never to be a priority for any administration which he headed. With so many wounds to heal, he did not intend to permit any imprudent public scrutiny of the rape of Cyprus.

History must pose the question, were American motives misplaced? A long peace has settled over Cyprus, which remains firmly within the Western orbit. Makarios limped home, but emasculated of any further capacity to cause trouble to the Great Powers. The British remained safely entrenched in their two sovereign areas, vital staging posts in the event of large-scale combustion in the Middle East. The United States controls a strategic base in the quasi-independent Turkish Cypriot northern zone, under the guise of a new civil airport. In twelve years, not a drop of Turkish or Greek Cypriot blood has been spilt. The sun-tanned UN troops who patrol the 'green line' separating the two communities serve in what locals are pleased to call 'the holiday army'. The Greek Cypriot canton in the south, for all its claims to represent a republic of the whole island, has enjoyed an unprecedented economic boom while prudently distancing itself from a closer embrace by the 'national centre' in Athens. The Turks, despite the relative economic poverty within their own enclave, have achieved a respectable degree of self-determination and independence under Rauf Denktash. And despite episodic tantrums, the long cold war between Greece and Turkey has remained just that, and both countries have stayed in NATO. The chart-makers in Washington could argue that Cyprus has been 'taken out' as a potent and divisive issue in international relations, while other fratricidal communities – like Ulster and Sri Lanka – continue to stew with violent dissent. The difference is, of course, that Cyprus was always a crucial strategic touchstone, which made the gamble worthwhile. By comparison, broken hearts can bleed over tribal wars in other far-off places without invoking a mighty intervention to strike for stability. There are many people in Washington who insist that in two decades which saw so many humiliating reverses for American influence, Cyprus sparkled as a great foreign policy success. The price in lives was high – but another question hangs larger. Might that blood account have filled a reservoir in any other circumstances?

16 · Missing Persons

They marched away enduring a belief
Whose logic brought them, somewhere else, to grief.

— W. H. Auden

At 6.30 a.m. on 18 March 1980, a police underwater search unit plunged into the river Thames not far from Walton Bridge. The local newspaper, the *Surrey Comet*, had a strange tale to report in its weekend edition: 'Mystery surrounds the drowning of a couple at Cowley Sale, Walton, a well-known spot for courting couples, in the early hours of Tuesday morning.' After a five-hour search along the murky river-bed, the police discovered a Volvo saloon. Inside, they found the body of a woman trapped in the rear seat, and outside that of a man with his fingers caught in the driver's door. A police spokesman told a reporter from the *Comet*: 'We thought at first the couple had been trying to bump start the car but it turns out that it was an automatic which cannot be started in this way.' This was the epitaph of Aristotellis Kotsias, then aged thirty-three, the senior Olympic Holidays representative during Ann Chapman's trip to Greece nine years earlier. Ann's father was always convinced that Kotsias could have told him much more about his daughter's death. He was certainly one of the most enigmatic characters in the story, and the mystery of his own strange death in the river Thames that March morning was in keeping with all that had gone before.

In 1971, when Ann flew to Greece, Kotsias, a young man of twenty-four, had a senior position with Olympic Holidays. He was the company's operations manager responsible for all their locations and staff in Greece while operating permanently from the London headquarters in Queensway. He was always insistent that he and Ann met for the first time when she arrived in Corfu with the party of travel agents. That was his story at the first trial of Moundis and again when he was interviewed by an inspector from Scotland Yard in 1977 as the moves to free Moundis were gathering pace. Kotsias said he was instructed over the phone from London to provide Ann with 'any assistance that she requires'. Ann's first request was indeed startling: it was for nothing less than an interview with the imprisoned Lady Amelia Fleming. Kotsias declared afterwards that he had 'not appreciated' the political significance of Ann's request, which seems remarkable, since the detention of Lady Fleming by the military regime had sent out shock-waves far beyond Greece. He was either blindly naive or he simply did nothing about Ann's request in order to avoid compromising Olympic Holidays in a highly provocative venture. Kotsias was supposed to be nurse-maiding a group of travel agents intent on boosting the Greek holiday business; yet here was a young BBC radio reporter asking for an entrée to one of the best-known opponents of the Colonels. Kotsias never explained, and, pertinently, seems never to have been asked, what kind of contacts he could have used to comply with Ann's request. Nor did he say if he had warned Ann of the risks she was taking even by showing an interest in the troubles of Lady Fleming. It is extraordinary that Kotsias should brush off the incident as though it were a trivial irrelevance, particularly as he had been alerted at an early stage of the trip to Ann's interest in controversial matters which were unlikely to bring much

191

comfort to his Olympic bosses in London. This explains a good deal about the subsequent behaviour of Kotsias when Ann went missing from the Pine Hill Hotel. It also indicates that he was acutely aware of the reasons for her strange conduct during that short stay on Corfu, so unnerving that Lynda Nichol had insisted on separate accommodation once the party reached Athens because Ann was 'too introverted and anti-social'.

Witnesses among the party of travel agents later recalled how Kotsias had first shown some surprise when Ann did not appear for dinner in downtown Athens on 15 October and how, on the following day, he exhibited increasing signs of anxiety and unease over her failure to reappear at the Pine Hill Hotel. Kotsias knew perfectly well that Ann's interest in the trip went far beyond the narrow confines of promoting tourism. He offered a vital clue about this during his interview with Scotland Yard when he admitted those anxieties were serious because Ann 'always telephoned if she was going to be late'. This time Ann did not telephone. Yet throughout that long weekend from 15–18 October, as rumour and speculation mounted among the group, Kotsias reported nothing to Olympic Holidays in London, still less to the BBC. He may have assumed that the police, who put out an all-points call on Saturday evening concerning Ann's disappearance, would be responsible for that. But Kotsias was not a junior courier, he was Olympic Holidays' senior representative on the spot in Greece, faced with the dreadful probability that something unpleasant had happened to a member of his party.

On Monday when the party flew to Crete, Kotsias left the unfolding crisis behind him; yet still no word reached Olympic Holidays in London that one of their passengers was missing. Before leaving, Kotsias asked Lynda Nichol and Shirley Butler to pack up Ann's belongings remaining in room 51. He supervised the operation and spotted that several of the tapes

Ann had with her appeared to be missing. He was also curious about a syringe, which he assumed was connected in some way with drugs, although he saw no sign of drugs anywhere in the room. The post-mortem produced no evidence of drug abuse. Kotsias, it is true, did not claim that drugs were found in the room, although others did. But his statement serves to support those disturbing elements of disinformation about Ann's character which proliferated with generous official encouragement after her death. And, despite his firm denials, stories persisted for years which linked Kotsias with Ann. Some investigators put forward the theory that he was a carrier-pigeon for the resistance, taking messages to and from Greece on his regular commuter trips for Olympic Holidays. If that was indeed the case, his name would have been buried deep in the resistance files, probably in code, to avoid exposure. The movement may have been fractured and disorganized but nevertheless many people – like Koutsoumbas, the booking clerk with Olympic Airways – operated for years under the noses of Greek intelligence without ever being detected. Kotsias certainly had many surface attractions for the resistance: he was young, fluent in English and could get in and out of Greece with ease, using his job as perfect cover. It is inconceivable that he was never approached to serve in the fight against the junta. He was also precisely the kind of young Greek attracted to haunts like the Troubadour in Earl's Court. When Kotsias went to his death in the river Thames in 1980, he took the answers to all these questions with him.

After the collapse of the junta, Kotsias stayed in London and gradually left the travel business. By the age of thirty-three, he had done remarkably well and seemed the epitome of the successful young émigré. He had an attractive home in Walton-on-Thames where he owned a restaurant and also sat on the board of a small local engineering company. He married and had two children. But his death, like that of Ann Chapman nine years before, remains invested with riddles.

On the evening of 17 March 1980, Kotsias drove to a popular riverbank pub, the Duke's Head, just a short distance downstream from Walton Bridge. He either took with him or met there Mrs Diane Wallwork. They chatted over drinks with mutual friends and left together at closing time. The landlord, who knew them both as popular and regular customers, thought they seemed 'perfectly normal'. In other words, neither was the worse for drink, a fact confirmed by the post-mortems. The couple may have sat talking in Kotsias' automatic Volvo, because it was not until just after midnight that two passing motorists observed bizarre events at the Duke's Head. Both later described at the coroner's inquest how a single car waltzed dramatically around the car-park, at one point crashing through a barrier on to the main road, and missing by inches one of these passing cars, driven by a woman. Both drivers also noticed the figure of a man who seemed to be conducting this strange drama, waving his arms wildly. The inquest heard how one of the motorists was sufficiently alarmed to drive back to the scene later. He found the car-park empty, the protective barriers guarding the roadside and the river smashed, and tyre tread marks leading straight to the water. The police were summoned and arrived within minutes. The underwater search unit quickly followed, on the assumption that the car seen careering madly around the Duke's Head car-park was now somewhere at the bottom of the river Thames. Frogmen plunged in almost immediately but did not locate the car for practically five hours. The Thames was in flood and the car had been carried a considerable distance downstream by strong currents. The body of a man – Kotsias – was trapped on the outside, his hand caught in a door. In the rear seat Mrs Wallwork was found, swept there from the front seat, the police thought, by the pressure of water as the car sank to the river-bed. The car ignition was switched on, with the gears in the automatic drive position. A single lady's shoe was lodged under the brake pedal and a handbag found in the passenger well. Kotsias was pulled out wearing just his trousers and a striped shirt. His shoes were discovered on a nearby riverbank pontoon.

When the coroner returned a verdict of death by drowning on Kotsias and Diane Wallwork, the inference was that after leaving the pub – about an hour before midnight on 17 March – Kotsias decided to give his friend a driving lesson. Neither were apparently deterred by the fact that automatic cars are notoriously difficult to drive by the inexperienced, and Mrs Wallwork was certainly that. Her former husband testified at the inquest that his ex-wife possessed virtually no driving skills whatsoever. Her provisional driving licence had run out in the early sixties and he was quite sure she never sat behind the wheel of a car again. Both Kotsias and Diane Wallwork had left the Duke's Head in good humour but not under the influence of drink. Yet, in the absence of any better explanation, she and Kotsias sat around in the car-park until all the other customers had left and then commenced a midnight driving lesson, with Kotsias – the figure waving his arms so wildly – offering tuition from outside the car. The risk of such an enterprise, particularly at a location only yards from a fast-flowing and deep river, was so obvious that Kotsias seems hardly the type of individual to court such dangers. Police experts who examined the vehicle were confident it entered the water with the engine running. They also noted one other curious fact: the rear nearside tyre was flat, punctured by an embedded nail. Kotsias would appear to have driven to the Duke's Head unaware that his car had a flat tyre. Whatever did happen later that night in the car-park, it is certain that the Volvo smashed through the protective barriers and plunged headlong into the fast-flowing Thames. Kotsias tore off his shoes and dived in pursuit, desperately struggling to tear open the door of the car and free Diane Wallwork.

The inquest raised more questions than it solved. Edward

Chapman, who sat throughout it, was one of the few who knew of the chain of events which connected this seemingly inexplicable tragedy in the river Thames with the death of his own daughter in Athens nine years before. The link with Ann was not exposed during the coroner's hearing, and seems never to have featured in the police inquiries. Others did make the connection. The Surrey coroner who presided over the inquest, Lieutenant Colonel McEwan, wrote to me three years later declaring that several people claiming to represent the Greek press had approached him for copies of the papers dealing with the case. 'I have refused them all,' he declared. Viewed as a single isolated event, the drowning of Kotsias is just another death by misadventure. But woven into the story of Ann Chapman, it becomes another marker on a long trail studded with strange and often fatal coincidence.

Kotsias went to his death in water. Less than two years previously, a mysterious and unexplained fire claimed the life of a man who threatened to upset much of the evidence which sent Moundis to prison for the manslaughter of Ann. This time the location was Athens. In October 1978, the owner of a small art gallery in the crowded central area of the city, Ananias Tryfonidis, claimed that he had seen Ann alive in his shop with a young, fair-haired Greek, at the time she was supposed to be dead. Tryfonidis declared that, after seven years of silence, his conscience now forced him to speak out. Ann had visited his art gallery, just off Kondoulis Street, on the night of 16 October. She appeared there between 9.30 and 10 o'clock with the young Greek, and stayed for about an hour, drifting around and looking at the pictures. 'She told me in broken Greek that she was English and, if my memory doesn't deceive me, I think I offered her some little thing from the works of art . . . I am certain that the foreigner in question was the murdered English journalist, Ann Chapman.' How could he be so sure, he was asked by reporters. Tryfonidis replied that he recognized the girl from the pictures which appeared after her death in the Athens newspapers but decided at the time to say nothing. Yet the only photograph immediately available – and the one used in the Athens newspapers – was taken from her passport, and that showed a somewhat younger Ann before she underwent cosmetic surgery to alter the shape of her nose. The likeness was not compelling.

After giving a press conference, Tryfonidis marched straight off to the office of the public prosecutor to repeat his story. There he was not unreasonably asked why he had remained silent for so long. 'I let the storm of talk abate . . . now I see there is no margin for an innocent man who is in prison.' In fact, Tryfonidis made his statement shortly after Edward Chapman flew into Athens for another of his periodic confrontations with the Greek government. Speculation that Moundis was about to be freed was rife in the capital and Tryfonidis probably judged that he was safe from retribution if he spoke out now.

On the face of it, much of what Tryfonidis told the press and then repeated to the public prosecutor seems greatly at variance with all that is known about Ann. There is no evidence that she had even a smattering of Greek, although it is just possible she had picked up enough simple phrases during the trip to make polite conversation with Tryfonidis. More interesting was his account of the young Greek he was convinced escorted Ann to his gallery: good-looking, somewhere between twenty and thirty and dressed in light summer clothes. They both left, said Tryfonidis, in a 'gay mood'. The claims of Tryfonidis were splashed across the pages of all the main Athens newspapers, one of which chattered ecstatically about 'the bombshell' he had thrown into the case. The excitement he stirred up must be viewed, however, against the background of other events concerning Ann taking place at the same time, the sum of which had served to revive flagging interest in her fate. Edward Chapman had just completed a well-publicized visit to Athens, during which he vigorously demanded answers to what he called 'the many unanswered questions'. Theodoru had also been making headlines. The Supreme Court judges were shortly expected to rule on the appeal by Moundis for a re-trial and his lawyer told reporters that this time 'his long-drawn-out efforts and struggles will be justified and Moundis will be declared innocent'. As matters turned out, Theodoru was displaying excessive optimism. But it certainly appeared as if Greek public opinion was being prepared for a verdict that Moundis had not, after all, killed Ann Chapman. In this context, the claim by Tryfonidis that she had been in his art gallery with a handsome young Greek on the very night she died, seemed to fit perfectly with the anticipated exoneration of Moundis.

On close examination, however, everything which Tryfonidis said was highly circumstantial: even if she had been at his gallery, what other witnesses could he produce to support him? His excuses for keeping quiet – at least in the period after the junta had fallen – seemed extremely thin. And what of the question that Ann had spoken even broken Greek with him? Tryfonidis certainly knew much of the detail of the case and quite enough to appreciate that if Ann really had been in his gallery at the time he claimed, then Moundis had acquired an impressive new alibi. There is no record of just how seriously the public prosecutor took this claim, or whether any effective attempts were made by the police to investigate it. Perhaps, like many others, he threw another red herring into the story merely to supply some kind of promotional excitement for himself or his art gallery. Or he could well have been prompted to make his disclosure just at the moment that Theodoru expected a successful conclusion to his long campaign to free Moundis. But Tryfonidis cannot supply the answers to these questions: six months after making the claims which so excited the Athens press, Tryfonidis' home was burnt to the ground and he perished with it.

Among the Athens newspapers which vigorously reported the efforts of Theodoru and Edward Chapman was the right-of-centre daily, *Vraydini*. Its staff included the talented young journalist George Trangas, who regularly contributed well-researched investigation features designed to expose the cover-up which sent Nicholas Moundis to prison. The newspaper had long enjoyed a reputation for unfettered comment on public matters which annoyed and unsettled many in the Greek establishment. In the years of the Colonels, *Vraydini* often caused so much offence to the regime that it was frequently banned from the streets. Penetrating analysis of the apparatus of state remains rare in the Greek press, so the articles written by Trangas, turning over every stone in the affair of Ann Chapman, were not only unique but also the source of considerable discomfort to those who preferred that the entire business should now be forgotten. Trangas enjoyed substantial backing and encouragement from his editor, an old lion of the Greek press called George Athanassiades. He had always proved an untiring scourge of political chicanery.

Athanassiades knew that his style and reputation had earned enemies, but he still never flinched from carrying any story which was certain to jangle nerves in high places. So, when a young man came to the *Vraydini* office on the evening of 19 March 1983, asking to see the editor with a story 'I know will interest him', Athanassiades readily agreed to receive his visitor. A business acquaintance and friend of Athanassiades, appreciating that the conversation might be delicate, agreed to step outside. After a few minutes, the young visitor reappeared, saying he wanted to fetch some documents for the editor to see. He returned, holding a small bag, and left the door of the office slightly ajar. Through this small gap, the visiting businessman, Courcoubines, saw the visitor 'whispering something in the editor's ear'. Whatever he said shocked and alarmed Athanassiades. 'This cannot happen,' he cried out. Seconds later shots were heard. Athanassiades was felled by two bullets from a small pistol, one in the back of the head, the second in the left shoulder. Courcoubines was also shot three times as the assassin fled from the editor's office. He recovered after a long spell in hospital but Athanassiades' career ended there, at the age of seventy-one, in a pool of blood in his own office. Despite a nationwide hunt which eventually spread to Cyprus and brought in Interpol, the killer was never found. Within a few days the Athens police claimed to have discovered leaflets produced by an anarchist terrorist cell calling itself the 'Anti-Military Struggle', claiming full responsibility for the shooting. But the anarchists hit back, denouncing the claims as '*provocazia*' and the leaflets as blatant forgeries. The trail then went cold. The excellent *Times* correspondent in Athens, Mario Modiano, has often observed that terrorists are rarely detained for their crimes in Greece. The killing of Athanassiades, in the style reminiscent of a Chicago gangland murder, did more than silence the editor of a newspaper known for its integrity and attachment to the truth. It rippled once again the surface calm of a state where the impossible happens altogether too frequently.

As Edward Chapman has been told so often, Greek ministers of justice make much of their inability to 'interfere' in the judicial process. Even after the European Parliament adopted unanimously, in May 1984, the resolution prepared calling on the Greek authorities to clear up the case of Ann Chapman – based on my conclusion that Moundis was entirely innocent – the doors in Athens stayed firmly closed. Yet in private, if not in public, Professor George Manghakis was prepared to concede that 'much had gone wrong in the case of Miss Chapman'. To the world he adhered strictly to the official line that the issue remained closed until lawyers representing Moundis could persuade the Supreme Court of his innocence on the basis of 'new evidence'. After one lengthy discussion in the minister's private office early in 1985, I proposed a different approach: the minister should appoint a judge or a senior official from his own ministry to sift through all the papers concerning the case on a strictly non-judicial basis. Manghakis, who had been facing strong pressures from inside PASOK against further involvement, nevertheless appeared willing to consider the proposition sympathetically as a way of breaking the log-jam. He asked for time to think about the implications.

A general election was imminent and Manghakis was nervous about the risk of compromising himself and the government. The conservative opposition had already served warning that one of its main attacks during the campaign would be the claim that the socialist government was trying to turn the country into a one-party state by stuffing all government departments and agencies with its own appointees. Manghakis could see that any public commitment to the idea of an independent referee to examine the Chapman case again might be seized upon by the government's enemies as proof that it was openly pushing its nose into the highly sensitive preserves of the judiciary. In April, Manghakis wrote me a stern letter, copied to the President of the European Parliament, retreating from all he said during our talk in Athens. He even denied entertaining the idea of a non-judicial investigation and then added a toughly worded sentence designed to prove that the hands of PASOK were always clean before the courts. He wrote: 'I regret to say that any further steps from your part cannot be conceived otherwise but as an intervention in the most sensitive sector of our public interest, the independence of the judiciary.' Manghakis had clearly had his knuckles rapped behind the scenes. But, despite the public disclaimer he sent to the European Parliament, Manghakis proved as good as his word. Towards the end of April, a source with excellent contacts inside the justice ministry sent information to me that a former state prosecutor, George Thefanopoulos, had been called in by Manghakis and instructed to 'make a new investigation of the Chapman dossier'. The initiative followed directly on the heels of my own visit to Athens.

There was also a disturbing report that the Ministry of Foreign Affairs had ordered officials at the justice ministry to hand over all files dealing with the Chapman case, which looked suspiciously like an attempt to block the Manghakis initiative from another direction. He had tried to avoid overt concentration on the Chapman affair by including in the brief he sent to Thefanopoulos several more 'unsettled cases' for his consideration. In the event, there was no independent review of the Chapman files. Thefanopoulos was murdered in broad daylight while driving to his office. Witnesses spoke of a young man on a motor cycle firing several shots at point-blank range through the car window. This method of assassination was the hallmark of a terrorist group calling itself 'November 17th', inspiration for the name being derived from the date of the student uprising at Athens Polytechnic in 1973. Its motives seemed confused and purposeless. The police turned over dozens of homes belonging to people with known extremist opinions, without locating a shred of evidence to prove even the existence of 'November 17th'. In Athens, the cynical view quickly developed – based on the gloomy experience of the past – that agents of the state were loose on the streets with a licence to kill, concealing their activities beneath the cloak of an imaginary anarchist threat to the nation. It was certainly curious how the frequency of attacks and threats to prominent citizens accelerated as the general election approached, together with solemn warnings from the governing party over the dangers posed by 'anarchists and dissidents working against democracy'. However, when Thefanopoulos was gunned down in his car, 'November 17th' remained inexplicably silent. Responsibility was instead claimed by a movement calling itself the 'Democratic Anarchist Front', of which little had been previously heard. The similarity in favoured styles of execution and choice of victims was not lost upon those who were studying the outbreak of gun law in Athens. Neither was the strange inability of the police force to get to grips with this supposed threat to the democratic stability of Greece. As in the case of Athanassiades before him, the killers of ex-state prosecutor Thefanopoulos have never been found. Manghakis himself ceased to be Justice Minister in a government reshuffle in April 1986. Many believe he was insufficiently political to survive the brittle climate created by PASOK, and also that his sympathies with Edward Chapman shackled the prospects of any further promotion under Papandreou.

Over the years, the tally of death and inexplicable disappearance among those who had intimate connections with the Chapman affair continues to mount inexorably. Coincidence will not serve as an acceptable explanation in a matter already so deeply fissured by distortion and competing acts of conspiracy. There is one essential strand which links all four deaths examined in this chapter: the connection with Ann. In each case, the inevitable outcome was silence. The legal brain called in by Manghakis was murdered before his work could acquire significant value. A newspaper editor who published articles challenging the conviction of Moundis – and a good deal more which caused anger and resentment in high places – paid the ultimate price for exercising freedom of the press. Flames put an end to the life of a man who threatened to become a provocative nuisance by claiming he had seen Ann alive when she was supposed to be dead. And Kotsias drowned in an accident whose circumstances defied reasonable explanation. Thefanopoulos and Athanassiades were the obvious targets of selective political terrorism, rather than victims chosen at random by anarchist forces trying to pry loose the hinges supporting the state. The excuse supplied –

that they had been killed by destructive elements bent upon destabilization – belies the fact that if anarchism does exist as a force in Greece, then it is a recent and unnatural phenomenon. Contemporary history of the country is dominated by the gaping political chasms separating Left and Right, with no indication of any instrument of chaos calling a plague on both houses. As in all the countries located along Europe's political earthquake fault, the rim of the southern Mediterranean basin, assassination has always been a familiar weapon of both crude influence and revenge. Those who commissioned the killings of public figures like Thefanopoulos and Athanassiades did so with a precise motive.

Prime Minister Andreas Papandreou has recently had much resort to his belief in destabilizing forces which he thinks threaten Greece: his party, PASOK, even tried to suggest that an outbreak of forest fires which swept the country during the summer of 1985 could be blamed upon those who were working against the security of the nation. The opposition sharply retorted that if politically motivated arsonists were responsible, then Papandreou could well start by looking for people behaving carelessly with matches inside PASOK. Many people judged that this well-thrown dart found its mark in a highly sensitive area. George Trangas told me during the course of a long discussion over the martyrdom of *Vraydini*'s editor that such acts could well promote certain interests who were seeking to sharpen the polarity of Greek politics. He would not elaborate on who these interests might represent, but the inference was clear that political terrorism in Greece drew its inspiration not from disaffected anarchists, but instead from those who were working to a specific programme intended to maintain the alignment of Greek politics on a preconceived course; and that is a complete contradiction to any identifiable creed of anarchism. The clumsy and unsuccessful efforts of the police in tracking down the assassins is also revealing, because it indicates the impotence of any serious attempt to discover who or what might be attempting to undermine the government of the nation. Some observers like to blame this on simple incompetence in a police service hampered by the lack of effective training and a deep-rooted lack of professional motivation. Yet that is wholly insufficient to explain why it is that Greece – and Athens in particular – has become a virtual hunting ground for terrorists, while the police look on as hapless bystanders. No other country in Europe has managed to allow quite so many terrorists to slip unaccountably through the hands of the civil power.

The death of Tryfonidis falls into a different category. Perhaps an electrical fault or an accident with a cigarette was responsible for his untimely end. Such an explanation would look plausible if this individual had not stepped so publicly into the business of Ann Chapman, making assertions which compromised the conviction of Moundis. As already noted, much of what he said about Ann visiting his art gallery was hugely circumstantial. So, of course, was all the evidence which put Moundis behind bars. The trouble with Tryfonidis was his persistence, no matter what degree of credence those claims actually contained. Apart from Moundis' father-in-law, he was the only independent witness who ever came forward with evidence which might compromise the course which Greek justice had taken: had his claim been substantiated in any respect, it would represent the tip of an iceberg protruding to the surface above the vast bulk of conspiracy below. In 1976, two years after the collapse of the Colonels' regime, there were plenty of people in Athens who had an interest in silencing unwelcome challenges to the official verdict on Ann, either as freelances or as servants of a wider interest. Tryfonidis offered himself as a hostage to either. His death, six months after he made headlines in the Greek newspapers with a 'new revelation' about Ann Chapman, bears the hallmark of accident by design.

In trying to judge what happened to Kotsias and his friend,

Mrs Wallwork, it is important to examine the comment he made to curious friends who had been active in the resistance movement and wanted to know more about Ann Chapman. Kotsias told them not to ask questions because it was a 'very dirty business'. By 1980, Kotsias knew quite sufficient to make him an object of attention for those with sinister ambitions. If the former senior representative of Olympic Holidays in Greece had gone on to reveal more about the 'dirty business' involved in the Chapman affair, he was clearly going to pose a serious threat to the conspiracy. One source suggested to me that Kotsias stayed quiet because he was given money to do so, and then started to ask for more: bribes had already featured strongly with regard to Moundis, but if Kotsias had taken that route, he must have realized it could eventually lead to catastrophe. By all accounts, he was a sober individual with a calculating style, who intended to move on quickly up the ladder of achievement as a modest entrepreneur. There is nothing in what is known of his character to explain what appears to be the foolhardy venture of indulging in impromptu driving lessons, with a virtual novice behind the wheel, in a pub car-park at midnight. And even if he had suspended sound judgement to that extent, why should he compound the folly by allowing Diane Wallwork to practise on a car with a punctured tyre? One of the eyewitnesses that evening – the woman who narrowly escaped a collision – thought she might have seen not one but two people in the car careering wildly around the car-park. Kotsias himself was certainly outside it – because he had the opportunity to tear off some of his clothes and dive after the car as it plunged into the river. The most important statement about events of that night in March 1980 is the outcome – Kotsias, who clearly knew so much about how Ann met her death, went to his in yet another bizarre accident which bestowed that valuable bonus of silence.

17 · The Last Supper

I have a rendezvous with Death
At some disputed barricade.

—Alan Seeger

Like the pieces of a scattered jigsaw, the events of Friday 15 October 1971 require careful re-assembly to discover precisely what did happen to Ann Chapman when she walked out of the Pine Hill Hotel. Every attempt so far to unravel the mystery falters on the assumption that she left the hotel in a hurry, to dash the one hundred or so metres down the road to catch a bus into central Athens. This assumption is based on the remarks which Ann made to the reception staff at the hotel and also to the young travel agent from Manchester, Nicholas Clarkson, with whom she had travelled back to Kavouri in the late afternoon. Ann had spent most of her day in Athens preoccupied with a private itinerary which did not include the rest of the Olympic Holidays party. She met up with them after lunch, hitching a lift to the city centre on the bus which had taken the group to view the Acropolis and then broke off again before popping in to the brief reception hosted by Dimitri Lalelis at the offices of Aeolian Travel. During the course of this busy schedule, Ann arranged an important rendezvous later that evening, but not with the Olympic party who were due to meet together for the dinner arranged by Kotsias at the Electra Hotel.

Throughout the trip, Ann had been keen to maintain the fiction that she had gone to Greece purely to report on the fortunes of the tourist industry. Kotsias and, subsequently, Lalelis were the only ones who knew positively about her curiosity concerning other, more sensitive, political matters. While glasses of ouzo were being handed out at the Aeolian reception, she seemed bright and communicative, and even mentioned the visit of Spiro Agnew while chatting to Lalelis. Brian Rawson, who was shortly to achieve such a remarkable vanishing trick, hovered among the members of the party, dispensing hospitality and small-talk, almost certainly over-hearing Ann's remark about Agnew. She plainly seemed anxious to return to Kavouri alone. Her travelling companions planned to remain behind in Athens, where Lalelis had made arrangements for wash-and-brush-up facilities. Her mind preoccupied with thoughts about the rendezvous she had arranged, Ann would have welcomed the opportunity for undisturbed reflection during the ride back to Kavouri. But, at the last moment, Clarkson announced he was feeling queasy with a mild stomach upset. He opted for a quiet evening in the hotel, instead of another late and probably boisterous night on the town, and offered courteously to escort Ann back to the Pine Hill Hotel. For her, Clarkson's change of plan represented an irritating distraction and she demonstrated every sign of this during their short journey together, especially as he was persistently inquisitive about her own plans for the evening. They agreed to take the bus instead of a taxi and the conversation is recalled by Clarkson as stilted, mostly indifferent small-talk about her world travels, punctuated by periods of silence. Whatever Ann planned that evening she was not going to discuss it with Clarkson. As the bus rumbled on towards Kavouri, she let him believe that after changing at the Pine Hill, she would smartly turn around and head back into Athens for the supper party at the Electra.

Most accounts agree the pair arrived at the hotel between seven and seven-thirty, collected their keys from the desk at reception and went straight upstairs to their respective rooms. Clarkson now had the impression that Ann was in a considerable hurry. That being the case – if she really was planning to return to Athens – it was surprising that she failed to take the elementary precaution of immediately checking the bus timetable with the clerk at reception as soon as she arrived at the hotel. Instead, she hastened upstairs to room 51. There she discovered a fault with her watch, which was either slow or had stopped completely. With the minutes ticking away towards the assignation she had arranged outside the hotel, Ann remembered Clarkson had a room nearby on the same floor. So she called out to him from her balcony, not once but several times, urgently checking the time. Clarkson naturally still assumed she was anxious only not to miss the bus. One essential element of Ann's bathroom routine during the half hour or so that she spent in her room was a change of tampon, a feature which later assumed crucial significance in the post-mortem by helping to fix precisely the moment of her death.

Ann reappeared in reception wearing, according to the clerk, George Malavetas, a brightly coloured Chinese-style mini-skirt. Clarkson came down at the same time and made straight to the bar for a beer. This was a small area near reception, from which he had a good view of Ann and easily overheard her conversation with the clerk, Malavetas, and the hotel manager, Basil Kasimatis. With hindsight, the short discussion seemed contrived and designed to maintain the fiction, especially with Clarkson, that she was indeed returning to Athens. Less than an hour before, she had stepped off the suburban bus just a few metres from the hotel. So her first question to Kasimatis was certainly strange. She asked for the precise location of the bus-stop. And only now, after fretting so much in her room about time, did she actually make her first inquiry about the bus schedules. Kasimatis, who wanted to impart an air of efficiency to the delegation which could potentially attract so much business to the hotel, quickly offered Ann a lift to Athens in his own car. Surprisingly, if there was such a hurry to get to the Electra, Ann rejected this. People in a hurry generally accept lifts which spare them the inconvenience of waiting about at night for a bus, particularly in countries like Greece where the service is usually erratic. Ann then stepped out into the evening gloom, confident she had laid an effective but deceptive trail. On the following day, it would be easy to explain that she had changed her mind about going to the Electra or elected instead to take a quiet meal alone.

Clarkson and the two staff at the Pine Hill reception, manager Kasimatis and the clerk, Malavetas, have always been credited as being the last people to see Ann alive. This is because evidence from the taxi driver, Phytas, was deliberately sabotaged in order to secure the conviction of Moundis. Phytas had collected two fares from the taxi rank in Vouliagmeni, one of whom he dropped about a kilometre short of the hotel but the second remained in the cab and got out at Pine Hill. From what the pair had said to each other during the brief trip, Phytas judged them both to be locals, who were thoroughly familiar with the area. The young woman he was later willing to identify as Ann Chapman emerged from the hotel, evidently anticipating the encounter with his sole remaining passenger. But she was dressed in jeans or trousers and not a mini-skirt as described by the reception clerk, Malavetas. Clarkson, sipping beer at the hotel bar, thought Ann had left wearing a pair of trousers with a zig-zag pattern, the ones later found in her suitcase. One of the major hindrances to any crime investigation is getting witnesses to achieve a precise and accurate recall over styles of dress. Malavetas, who saw dozens of people passing through his reception area every day, had no particular reason

210

to make a careful note of Ann's clothes. When her body was discovered three days later, she was naked from the waist down, except for her pants. There was no trace of a mini-skirt of any description. Her torso was still, however, partially clothed in a light blouse, made from a cheese-cloth material and stamped with a noticeable pattern. This was a souvenir bought during Ann's holiday in Goa. When the search squad from the gendarmerie finally located most of Ann's belongings in the field adjacent to the bus stop, they found trousers similar to those described by Phytas. Malavetas had only a waist-up view when he saw Ann talking to the hotel manager at reception. With a virtually subliminal glance, he could easily have mistaken the bright Indian blouse with its striking design for a mini-dress. In contrast, Phytas had a full-length view of the young woman and her clothes and his description conformed with the clothes later found on and near the body. He was also quite sure that the girl who emerged said to his passenger 'Why are you late?', another telling indication of her preoccupation with making a date on time.

Ann's movements all day, like every step throughout her stay in Greece, had been closely monitored by the Greek intelligence services. If there was any truth to Moundis' claims that he saw policemen lurking outside the hotel, it could be that a car had been parked by a shadowing team somewhere in the woody scrubland. But his lurid tale of a young foreign woman being snatched literally from the doorstep of the hotel and forced, screaming, into an official-looking black car is no more than that. Ann saw no reason to fear whoever it was she stepped out so willingly to meet. The time was now shortly after eight o'clock, between three and four hours before Ann's death. Within the next two hours she ate a small traditional Greek snack, something like souvlaki, a small pitta bread sandwich containing meat. And Ann did not appear anywhere in Athens that evening. Instead, she was taken by car in the opposite direction, along the Sounion road, to the nearby village of Vouliagmeni. Along this route, Ann and her companion, the young man delivered in the taxi by Phytas, stopped at a small taverna where others joined them. The choice of Vouliagmeni for a quiet talk over a light meal is important. For some years a small block of flats not far from the tiny enclosed bay had served as a 'safe house' for members of the resistance movement, a useful staging post close to the airport and suitably distant from prying eyes in the bustling streets of Athens. The function of the flat in this small, anonymous resort was to allow resistance workers to meet and exchange messages and to rest up between operations. But the lair had long since been betrayed to the guardians of state security, who understood its role precisely. As the *Vraydini* reporter George Trangas told me pointedly: 'Some members of Democratic Defence were not what they seemed.' The junta's highly successful penetration of the resistance movement in Greece included the familiar technique of planting double-agents, whose task was aided immeasurably by the rivalry between the competing resistance factions. When Ann walked out of the Pine Hill Hotel on the night of 15 October, she stepped directly into the twilight world of treachery.

Before leaving London, Ann had been led to believe that a range of contacts to whom she would be introduced in Greece would lead her to a journalistic exposé. As Helen Vlachos later observed, it was theoretically easy for a British journalist visiting the country to produce a convincing story which could tell against the regime – hence Ann's wish to interview Amelia Fleming, which she conceived as an additional scoop to the main enterprise. What she utterly failed to appreciate was the risk of being drawn into the struggle between the junta and the resistance and, much worse, to perceive that either side would ruthlessly exploit her curiosity. Helen Vlachos thought it perfectly conceivable that Ann found herself lured into a fake anti-Colonels story manufactured by the regime in order to lead them to sources of opposition inside the country. The truth was a subtle variation on that theme. In London Ann had consorted with members of the resistance and a senior official at the Greek embassy, a trusted official of the regime specifically charged with the task of inquiring into the motives of foreigners, especially foreign journalists, visiting the country. In the event, she tapped into a story of such enormous potential impact that, inevitably, powers far more influential than Greek intelligence began to take an active interest in her plans.

Word of an impending solution to the problem of Cyprus, which would involve a dangerous act of complicity by the Colonels, had begun to circulate on the resistance telegraph early in 1971. The source of this leak was the Papandreou command post in Stockholm, which – via the Arne Treholdt connection – enabled Soviet detection of the scheme. At that time it seemed probable that the dramatic initiative was imminent. Realizing this could well precipitate the collapse of the military regime, resistance circles everywhere watched eagerly for any sign of movement. When it was announced by the junta that the American Vice-President, Spiro Agnew, would visit the country in mid-October, tension rose immediately. It was not a coincidence that Ann's plans to visit the country began to take shape and then harden as the October deadline for Agnew's visit drew closer. Radio London's young freelance reporter was a novice in the murky world of international conspiracy, so in the weeks before leaving, she packed her mind with every conceivable nugget of information about the country and what was happening there. The carefully annotated press clippings found after her death are proof of Ann's studied homework. She even researched the biographies of Basil Mantzos' co-directors on the board of Olympic Holidays and noted with interest that one, the Duke of St Albans, had an intelligence background. At the Troubadour, she was continually fed with appetising morsels

213

of information by the young Greek who always contrived to turn the conversation to Greek politics and against the Colonels. Clumsily, she opened a line of contact to 'eyes and ears' at the Greek embassy and, in that instant, sealed her fate. In the last moments before leaving Britain, Ann shuddered at the prospect of what she was doing, and almost unburdened those fears to her parents. But her determination to succeed and return from Greece with sensational revelations overrode all instincts which cried out for caution.

When she reached Corfu, Ann quickly perceived the extreme loneliness and exposure of her position. Where she went during that eighty-kilometre traverse of the island in the hired Fiat car can never be satisfactorily established, but the premeditation with which the journey was arranged in London suggests that the vehicle she rented contained instructions on how to commence contact with her promised informants. Hence the telling significance of the inscription in her diary: 'Find name of Fiat garage.' Ann was thoroughly unsettled during this initial experience of espionage, which explains her curious, distracted behaviour throughout the duration of her stay on Corfu. In Athens she pressed ahead, still nervous but confident she could ride through and get safely out of the country with her story.

Friday 15 October was the day on which she was due to link up with her most important contact in Athens. After so many preparations she found this at last exhilarating. At the Aeolian Travel reception her brimming confidence overflowed, allowing her to let slip the comment about Spiro Agnew's impending visit. Then Clarkson's tiresome stomach pains led to the fumbled excuses about returning to the hotel for a wash and change before a convivial night on the town with the others in the Olympic party. But Lalelis was sufficiently troubled by what he heard from Ann to telephone the BBC's official correspondent in Athens, Janet Damen, the following day – when he knew Ann was missing – to discover more about her curiosity concerning Agnew. Janet Damen, once she had spoken by telephone with the man she later discovered to be Dimitri Lalelis, would certainly have been prompted to make a precautionary check with the BBC's central newsdesk in London. Athens was, after all, her own 'beat' and it is one of the features of journalism that professionals on the spot dislike their feathers being ruffled by freelancers who turn up to root about on jealously-guarded territory. Ann, travelling incognito with a party of British travel agents, was a curious sort of figure to be displaying interest in the visit of Agnew. Damen – who had not been asked by London to file a report on the visit – would not want to court the risk of missing a story. But was the BBC's official woman on the spot in Athens really so surprised by Ann's arrival? Among the findings in the field at Kavouri was a scrap of paper bearing a scribbled note of Damen's address and telephone number. Whoever ransacked Ann's handbag and later scattered her belongings over the fabricated trail made the crucial mistake of ignoring the significance of this one fragment. In fact, Ann intended this possible link with Janet Damen as her lifeline to the world in the event of an emergency.

As Ann left the Pine Hill, the framework for potential assassination was all but complete; but since death is always the guardian of silence, the object of the exercise that evening was really to find out just how much she knew, and from whom. Patriots like Vassili Filias are naturally determined to defend the resistance movement operating inside the country against the accusation that it was riddled with junta spies: in reality, the mixture of well-meaning academics and intellectuals, seasoned with earnest and genuine adventurers like Martin Packard, was no match for powerful agencies backed with the might of the CIA. Filias, however, did admit to me that by 1971 resistance cells in Greece had been virtually wiped out by the regime's security forces. Opposition to the junta had almost ground to a halt, thanks almost entirely to the well-oiled machinery feeding Greek intelligence with advance information on every potentially subversive enterprise originating outside the country.

The young Greek whom she met outside the hotel spoke Greek and English with a tinge of an American accent. At the taverna in Vouliagmeni the pair were joined by the other passenger Phytas had picked up in his taxi, and then deposited a short distance from the Pine Hill. Transport to Vouliagmeni was almost certainly provided in the white Morris car which had been hovering in the area, and whose occupants were obviously familiar with the taxi passengers. The brief conversation which Phytas described to the gendarmerie was concerned with arrangements to collect Ann and her contact. From the start she was encouraged to feel safe and trusted among friends. After the light snack at the taverna, Ann and at least two of her confidants headed to the safe house at the apartment block. There she was offered more drink in an attempt to ease more information from her; but the 'nice' part of the technique was soon to give way to the thoroughly nasty. Ann was both stubborn and, by now, suspicious and very alarmed. This provoked the combination of anger and frustration which propelled her inevitably across the frontier dividing survival from death. The earlier harmony of the evening was shattered. She was held in a chair and slapped and beaten around the face, probably with blows from a fist – as Kapsaskis proposed in his post-mortem – or perhaps some kind of 'blunt instrument'. When this treatment failed to produce co-operation, there were threats that she would never leave the place alive. Indeed, after what had already happened she could never be allowed to do so. She was already in need of medical attention, bleeding badly from the nose, unable to see clearly. Even with the extraction of a promise to keep quiet, her condition itself told a damning story. In the closing seconds of her life, she was struck in the

216

lower chest with considerable force, probably by a knee, an act which fractured a rib. It is probable that at this point, excruciating pain and hysteria stunned Ann's senses and mercifully allowed her to slip into unconsciousness. Still seated in the chair, she was then gripped firmly from the rear by the forearms, leaving those indelible bruises found by Kapsaskis, and then slowly throttled by a right-handed man with a terrifying grip.

18 · The Price of Conspiracy

Truths would you teach, or save a sinking land?
All fear, none aid you, and few understand.

Alexander Pope

Ann Chapman was murdered between midnight and one o'clock on the morning of Saturday 16 October. For at least seven hours, perhaps an hour or two longer, her body lay face up on the floor of the apartment, blood gradually clotting to form the tell-tale condition of hypostasis. The frightful reality of this clumsy and potentially extremely costly blunder now confronted the killers. As morning broke, the Olympic party would inevitably become aware she was not in the hotel. And within a very short time from the discovery of an empty room 51, the police and gendarmerie would be forced to react to a report concerning a missing foreign journalist. As daylight approached, the task of moving a dead body away from the incriminating environs of the apartment at Vouliagmeni became increasingly fraught with hazardous and complex difficulties. Ann's body must be shifted – but where? The most immediate and pressing necessity was to find a sufficiently plausible location, whose circumstance would, in itself, advance some kind of motive for a suspicious and clearly brutal death. This supposedly subtle exercise had gone disastrously wrong; the hunters were now, by implication, the hunted. This ruled out any possibility of an appeal for help which would obviously entail the risk of serious political compromise. While rigor mortis gradually froze Ann's corpse into the gruesome posture of death, the minutes and hours elapsed. The sum of all that followed from then on amounts to an extraordinary shambles. Whatever had to be done with the body must be done under cover of darkness. The passage of ten to twelve hours would be required to get the body out of the flat, to take advantage of the veil of advancing night on Saturday evening; alternatively, the present cloak of darkness could be exploited. This last course posed the risk of early risers spotting a stiff and cumbrous object being lugged out of the apartment block. Whatever sense of caution now existed dictated more time to contrive an exercise which should provide a satisfactory explanation for murder. None of those present knew that every move they made left forensic markers all over Ann's body. Between eight and nine o'clock on Saturday morning, the corpse was shifted into a different position, face down, the profile in which it would eventually be discovered by the snail-gatherers. As Kapsaskis would observe precisely during his autopsy, hypostasis was only partially formed from the original position in which the body lay.

Throughout Saturday, word of Ann's fate permeated the innermost counsels of the Greek intelligence organization. Word had been despatched to Vouliagmeni from the highest level that on no account was news of the discovery of Ann's body to make a provocative junction with the arrival of Spiro T. Agnew, Vice-President of the United States of America. Therefore, the early hours of Sunday morning were selected for the pretence of displaying the body at a location conceived suitable for its discovery. This was to be the field alongside the main road at Kavouri, close to the stop serviced by the buses to and from Athens.

An inexorable 'rule of three' appreciated by all pathologists governs the condition of every corpse in the immediate hours

219

following death. By applying this rule to the events that weekend, it can be clearly seen how the conspirators made their moves. In the initial twelve hours from death, rigor mortis gradually advances, solidifying the corpse. For the next twelve hours, this condition is fixed, posing serious difficulties for movement. Finally, after the elapse of a third period of twelve hours, suppleness gradually returns to the limbs, permitting a body to be shifted about with relative ease though it is still – as the appropriate phrase describes – a 'dead weight'. By the time Ann was taken from Vouliagmeni, her body was in the final phase. In other words, she had been dead for more than twenty-four hours and the task of moving her was simplified by the gradual evaporation of rigor mortis. Either now – or later in the field at Kavouri – her wrists and ankles were secured with wire. Then, as Kapsaskis noted so pertinently, two individuals carried Ann, one gripping her by the knees, the other at the shoulders. A five-minute journey by car along the main road to Athens brought the macabre party to the crossroads at St Nicholas. A suitable spot for discovery somewhere within the chosen location now had to be selected. Too near the road and the bus stop would prompt premature discovery and the possibility of some compromising link between the dead journalist and the recent arrival of Agnew. She was therefore manhandled over the low wall and manoeuvred into a face-down position, on a slight rise in the patch of land, a metre or so from the rough, stony track bordering the north of the site. The elements of a precisely organized, carefully considered exercise in deceit were all glaringly absent. In the first instance, Ann's trousers had been tugged off to suggest a sexual motive for the attack: but in the general confusion the trousers were left behind at Vouliagmeni and were only to manifest themselves five days after the body was found. Also overlooked were virtually all of Ann's belongings, including her handbag, shoes and other crucial items she had taken out of the Pine Hill Hotel with her on Friday evening. However, the conspirators did scatter her passport, memo book and a few other small possessions, but on the wrong side of the wall, in the direction from which the corpse had been hauled from the boot of a car. Everything was hurried and ill-considered, partly through fear of interception – even in those small dark hours – and also out of cold fear of intimate contact with death. The last act was to scatter a few ragged scraps of rough grass over the corpse to imply a suitably clumsy attempt at concealment. As the dawn broke over Kavouri and the Greek coastline, bringing in its wake a hostile day of torrential rain, the stage had been perfectly set for a crime that never was.

But this was the beginning and not the end. Like a door banging constantly, the truth about Ann's death demanded to be heard. Her visit to Greece had thrown her into the embrace of individuals who served two masters. The real tragedy of Ann Chapman lay in that sublime act of innocence with which she gave up her life to those who cynically manipulated and exploited the desires of a people to be free. On that fateful October evening in 1971, she was savagely beaten and then cold-bloodedly murdered by agents of the state who posed before her as opponents of that same regime. Those people, as I told the European Parliament, are alive in Greece today, still the principal guardians of a conspiracy which has gone on for fifteen years. They have been protected from retribution and justice by successive Greek governments who are reluctant to raise even one tiny corner of the curtain concealing this affair for fear of exposing to public glare the compromising activities of prominent men – and a judgement of shame on what they did during a tawdry and disgraceful episode of Greek history. Ann remains a silent martyr to this bitter cause because her parents were abandoned by all who could have led them to the truth. The price of conspiracy has been deceit, distortion, the imprisonment of an innocent man and the cruel anguish of Ann's parents.

Edward and Dorothy Chapman have paid that price in full.

Postscript

In the autumn of 1986 I met another witness who had talked
with Ann shortly before her death, a young Greek girl who
had previously worked for a subsidiary of the Mantzos organization in London and was now an extra hand at the offices
of Aeolian Travel in Athens. The encounter between the two
was brief – although they also had a passing acquaintance in
London – but during a short stroll around the shops, Ann
declared she was positive 'eyes are following me everywhere'.
This witness, who is now absorbed into one of the vast
international institutions in Brussels, is still reluctant to put
her own name to her testimony. Subsequent events make
this not surprising. In the wake of Ann's death, she was
precipitately fetched from home in a police squad car and
spent the best part of three days under interrogation, including
one disturbing period lasting for hours abandoned in a fea-
tureless room staring at the blank walls. This may have been
a unique example of attention to detail during the police
inquiry, but the entire episode strikes only alarming notes.
The police asked few questions but were adamant that their
greatly perturbed young guest was wrong in claiming that Ann
had been wearing sandals and had with her a shoulder-bag
containing her small portable tape recorder.

During a long discussion over dinner in Brussels, 'Miss X'
said she was later surprised not to have been summoned to

222

the trial of Moundis. But then, a witness who would speak of Ann's certainty that she was being tailed all over Athens could only have proved an alarming intruder at the stage-managed conviction of an innocent man. Her evidence about Ann's clothing – plus of course any reference to compromising official curiosity about Ann's tape recorder – ensured her exclusion from the proceedings, since it had been clearly established in those early days that she could only prove hostile. Fifteen years after Ann's death, more proof had surfaced of the bungling which went on to supply a plausible explanation of how Ann Chapman came to be found lifeless in the field at Kavouri.

Index

225